1

Little Known Tales In Hawaii History

By Alton Pryor

Stagecoach Publishing
5360 Campcreek Loop
Roseville, CA. 95747
stagecoach@surewest.net

Little Known Tales In Hawaii History

Copyright © 2003 by Alton Pryor

Library of Congress Control Number:
2003099556

ISBN: 9780974755113

Stagecoach Publishing
5360 Campcreek Loop
Roseville, California 95747
stagecoach@surewest.net
www.stagecoachpublishing.com

Little Known Tales In Hawaii History

By Alton Pryor

Stagecoach Publishing
5360 Campcreek Loop
Roseville, CA. 95747
stagecoach@surewest.net

Table of Contents

Preface

One doesn't just visit Hawaii. A trip to these magical islands is to learn a new life-style.

Hawaii is a cultural and ethnic phenomenon. It has its native Hawaiians, but there are Caucasian, Chinese, Japanese, Portuguese, Okinawan, Korean, Filipino, Samoan, Vietnamese, and Hmong. If we've left you out, you have our sincere apologies.

One of the author's greatest experiences was the four years he spent there while in the U.S. Navy. He visited a working cattle ranch at Kona on Hawaii, where he spent three days in the company of a *paniolo*, a term for a Spanish cowboy. The Hawaiian cowboys adopted the term to describe themselves.

In a later trip, I toured the Parker Ranch, and interviewed its foreman for a story I was doing for a California magazine.

There were trips to the beaches, to waterfalls where one had to walk up paths in lush rain forest type foliage. Lei Day (May 1) is a time that no island visitor should miss.

Four years in Hawaii was not enough. Perhaps a lifetime is not enough. We hope you enjoy some of the Hawaiian heritage we are passing your way. —Alton Pryor

14

Chapter 1

The Menehunes:
Hawaii's 'Little' People

Kalalau Valley, Kauai

Hawaii is populated by a magical group
of little people called Menehunes. The
little people are noted for their skilled
stonework, the building of waterfalls, irrigation
waterways, and fishponds.

If legend is correct, the Hawaiians on Kauai
descended from two different races, the
Polynesians and the Menehunes. The Polynesians
were tall, but the Menehunes were only about

three feet tall, and were well established on Kauai when the Polynesians arrived.

The Menehunes multiplied to the point their population reached 500,000 Menehune men. One belief is that the Menehunes are very shy and do most of their good work during the middle of the night when they can't be seen. To see them, a person must be a descendant of the little people or consume a special juice or potion to see them.

Others say the Menehunes are so small they fly about on the backs of seagulls. The Menehunes carry tiny horns around their necks. These are used to signal the seagulls when they are in trouble.

People who aren't able to see the Menehunes sometimes hear the hum of their voices. The Menehunes are the protectors of Hawaii and its inhabitants.

Legend notes that in years past, a huge wave was descending towards Hawaii and the King of the Menehunes began blowing his horn. Menehunes came running from all over the island and formed a line by holding hands.

The small, but powerful, Menehunes so terrified the wave that it broke up and became Kaneohe Bay.

The Menehunes protect the islands from sharks as well. They beat the sharks with their paddles until they swim away.

Menehunes were prodigious workers. By the light of the moon they built huge stonewalls, irrigation ditches and enclosures for ponds. They were shy, however, and if they were interrupted during their nocturnal labors, they would flee to the mountains, leaving the job undone.

On Kauai today, tourists are shown the Alakoko Fishpond at Niumalu as an example of the Menehunes unfinished work. The Menehunes always left the task they were performing when they were being spied upon.

One story tells of a Hawaiian chief and his sister who contracted with the tiny people to build enclosures for two fishponds. The work for the chief was completed in one night but the walls for the sister's pond was not finished because the Menehunes were frightened away.

Another object of the little people's work is the Menehune Ditch in Waimea Valley. This watercourse is operational. Its finely hewn walls are typical of Menehune craftsmanship. The walls were constructed in one night as the Menhunes passed rocks hand over hand for a distance of five or six miles.

People left the Menhunes delectable edibles as rewards. Included was a shrimp, the main item of the Menehune diet, coconut pudding and sweet potatoes.

When the first census was taken on Kauai in the 1850s, sixty-five people listed their racial background as Menehune.

Chapter 2

The Ukulele Arrives in Hawaii

These stacked ukulele bodies are ready to have necks, bridges and tuning keys added. (Google Images)

The ukulele was not invented in Hawaii. It was invented by three Portuguese immigrants coming to Hawaii aboard the *Ravenscrag* to work in the sugar cane fields. Master craftsman Manuel Nunes, with help from his Portuguese colleagues, Joao Fernandes, Jose do Espirito Santo, and Augustine Dias, designed the ukulele (oo-koo-le-le).

Using basic designs of instruments found in their native Portugal, Nunes and his colleagues invented the ukulele. While its origins are not Hawaiian, its history in the islands has made it so.

When the immigrant ship docked in Honolulu, Joao Fernandes grabbed his friend's *braguinha* (Portuguese name for the ukulele), jumped from the ship to the wharf and started playing folk songs from his native land. Hawaiians flocked to the docks, enchanted by the music from the flying fingers of Fernandes.

Manuel Nunes
Inventor of the ukulele.

The Hawaiian word *Ukulele* translates into "jumping flea" in English. This was the image conjured up by the flying fingers of Fernandes. Other translations of the name *ukulele* vary. The ukulele brought to Hawaii by Nunes was made of pinewood. The top was left unpolished so it would have a better sound. It was handmade.

Queen Lili'uokalani believed *ukulele* came from the Hawaiian words "the gift that came here", or "uku" (gift or reward) and "lele" (to come). Still another translation is that the instrument was originally called "ukeke lele or "dancing ukeke" (ukeke being the Hawaiian's three stringed musical bow."

Another version is attributed to Gabriel Davian and Judge W.L. Wilcox, who was a member of a well-known island family. This story says the two men were in attendance at a housewarming party at the Wilcox home in Kahili, where Davian was playing a ukulele he had made himself.

When one of the guests asked what it was called, Davian jokingly replied that, judging from the way one "scratched at it," it was a "jumping flea." When Wilcox was asked for the Hawaiian translation, he answered, "ukulele."

Over the years, the instrument's name was most often mispronounced and almost universally became known as "ukulele."

The Hawaiian people quickly adopted the ukulele. The ukulele was easy to learn, small, and portable.

Hawaii's King David Kalakaua learned to play the ukulele. He was known as the Merry Monarch. He ascended the throne of the Hawaiian Kingdom in 1874 and reigned until his death 1891.

King David was a patron of the arts, especially music and dance. He restored many of the nearly extinct cultural traditions of the Hawaiian people, including its myths and legends, and the "hula", which had been forbidden by the missionaries for more than 70 years.

The hula was the means by which the culture, history, stories and almost every aspect of Hawaiian life was expressed and passed down through generations.

A great demand developed for ukuleles. Augusto Dias opened a shop on King Street in Honolulu to make and repair musical instruments, especially guitars and ukuleles. Four years later, Nunes and Santos opened musical repair shops.

Of the three, Nunes was the most successful, as he and his son Leonardo made ukuleles into the 1930s. Orders for "ukes" grew so numerous Nunes could not keep up with the demand. Nunes took in a young apprentice named Samuel Kaialilii to help him keep up with the orders.

The young apprentice in turn became very successful. In 1916 Kaialilii opened the Kamaka Ukulele and Guitar Works in Honolulu. His sons, Sam and Fred, joined the operation in 1941. In 1968 the firm incorporated in the name Kamaka Hawaii, Inc.

Early ukulele making was a painstaking art. It required hours of work to hand-make a ukulele. Ukuleles at that time sold for between $3 and $5, a large sum when many people made only $5 per month in salary.

People who could not afford to purchase a ukulele sometimes made their own out of coconut shell halves, cigar boxes, and other unusual material.

Chapter 3

Captain Cook Hawaii

Captain James Cook

The Hawaiian Islands are the summits of the world's tallest mountain range. The range towers 32,000 feet above the ocean floor. No one really knows from where the first Polynesians came that occupied Hawaii

Captain James Cook, born in Yorkshire, England, was first, after the Polynesians, to discover Hawaii. Cook wasn't looking for these magical islands. He was searching for the mythical Northwest Passage that led from Europe to

Asia. Cook made the discovery in 1877 as he sailed his two ships, the *Resolution* and the *Discovery,* from the Society Islands to the Arctic.

The first sign that land was near were sightings of tropical birds. Cook jotted this occurrence in his journal in a rather unexcited manner. "All these are looked upon as signs of the vicinity of land," he wrote.

Cook and his crew had found the islands of Oahu, Kauai and Niihau, the pearls of the Hawaiian Archipelago. As Cook's vessels headed toward Kauai, the "floating forests" caused great excitement among the islanders.

Canoes thronged from offshore to greet them. The oarsmen wore only loincloths.

Captain Cook recognized the dialect of the canoe occupants as one he had learned in Tahiti. To appease the natives as they came to his ships, Cook tied brass medals to a rope and lowered them as gifts to the brown-skinned men. The islanders, in return, tied small fish on the rope in return. Thus began the bartering process.

A brisk trade soon built up between the English and the natives. The natives traded hogs, sweet potatoes and fresh water for nails and pieces of iron. The islanders liked anything made of iron.

They gladly provided enough pork to feed the ships' crew for a day for a few small nails. The natives were astute. They envisioned the nails as ideal materials to fashion into fishhooks.

At this period in their history, the eight islands of Hawaii were governed as four separate independent chiefdoms. The lush northern island of Kauai and its smaller neighbor, Niihau, were under one ruling chief. Oahu and Molokai were a second chiefdom. A third chiefdom included three islands, Lanai, Maui and sparsely populated Kahoolawe. The fourth and largest chiefdom was *Havaiki*, which today is called Hawaii.

The Hawaiians considered high chiefs descendents of gods, and they ruled their people with absolute authority. When a high chief walked by, commoners prostrated themselves. It was *kapu* (forbidden) for one to allow his shadow to fall on the house, much less the person, of a high chief. Violation of these *kapu* brought instant death by war club or strangulation.

Drawing of the death of Captain Cook.
(Google Images)

One strong *kapu* was that women could not eat in the company of men. It was *kapu*, too, for

25

women to eat pork, bananas, coconuts, turtle meat and certain kinds of fish, but these same items were perfect fare for the men.

The chief who could trace his lineage most directly to the gods was king. He might rule an island or part of an island. All lands belonged to him and he appointed lesser chiefs to serve as governors for sections of his kingdom.

The sails of the big ships commanded by Captain Cook reminded the natives of the billowing cloth sheets of the *makahiki* god and so they treated Cook like a god.

The natives on the islands believed Cook was a fabled king of Hawaii named *Lono*, and that he had returned after a long absence. According to legend, *Lono* had killed his wife in a fit of anger. He had gone mad with grief, and spent his years wandering through the islands boxing and wrestling with anyone he met.

Finally, he set out in a canoe, aimed for foreign lands, and his people made him a god. In his honor annual games were held in the season of *makahiki* (the harvest season).

The islanders hailed Captain Cook as the god *Lono*. He and his crew were supplied with hogs, sugar cane, coconuts and breadfruit. In return, he gave the natives some of the two-foot iron daggers shaped by the blacksmith aboard the *Resolution*.

The British crew gave the islanders even more lasting gifts, those of syphilis and gonorrhea, which had a major affect in depleting the population of these serene people.

Cook's vessels were abundantly fitted with the iron the island men adored. The islanders made frequent attempts to steal the coveted material at any chance. This kept crewmen alert when they were on board.

Word of Lono's return spread throughout the islands. When the *Resolution* and the *Discovery* sailed into the sheltered bay of Kealakekua at Kona, the ruling chief, Kalaniopuu, hurried to greet the visitor that the islanders considered sacred.

The British sailors preoccupation with sex aroused the suspicions of Kalaniopuu. He put a *kapu* (Taboo) on women visiting the two ships. The crewmen then thronged to shore and took the women and girls in the villages.

It was when Captain Cook, with his ships now loaded with provisions, attempted to leave, that the natives realized he could not be the god Lono. They arrived at this conclusion when one of Cook's vessels was besieged by a storm off Kohala. The foremast of the Resolution was severely damaged. The captain and his crew had to return to the island to repair the damage.

This meant the captain and his crew were mere mortals and not gods at all. The natives then stole one of Captain Cook's long boats. The irate Captain decided to take Chief Kalaniopuu hostage until the longboat was returned.

When Cook attempted to arrest Kalaniopuu, a warrior protecting his chief struck Cook a heavy blow. Cook reeled and cried out in pain. The Hawaiians duly noted that if he could be hurt and cry out in pain he was no god.

The islanders struck him with more blows, causing him to fall into the shallows at the rocky edge of the bay. A bit of irony accompanied his death. The sea captain had never learned to swim.

Cook's crewmen shot and killed several Hawaiians before swimming back to the safety of their ships.

The Hawaiians then bestowed their highest honors on Cook's remains, and the tension lessened. They returned Cook's bones to the British, who gave them a Christian burial.

Chapter 4

Hawaii's Wondrous Money Tree

Sandalwood tree

Hawaii was in dire financial straits. King Kamehameha recognized that he needed a product to attract world trade to his peaceful islands. While the islanders had become proficient at raising fruits and vegetables, little cash could be obtained by selling provisions.

Even the oyster beds, which Kamehameha had cultivated at the mouth of the Pearl River, failed to bring in the income the kingdom needed.

In the forests of the Hawaiian Islands grew a tree that the natives called *iliahi*. It is an aromatic and fragrant wood used for carving religious idols, fancy boxes, and other items. The Hawaiians used sticks of it to make bows for their musical instruments. The natives ground the

29

wood and sprinkled it on kapa cloth clothes as a perfume.

Westerners recognized the iliahi as sandalwood. In the 1780s, fur traders, who had found a market for their hides in Canton, noted that there was a good demand there for sandalwood. Two merchant captains soon dropped men off at the Sandwich Islands to harvest this magnificent wood growing there.

The traders, however, made a huge mistake. The quality of the wood they first took to Canton was so poor the Chinese would not buy it. Consequently, the sandalwood trees in Hawaii were left alone for the next twenty years, while the same wood on other islands in the southwest Pacific was exploited.

In 1810, three American traders, William Heath Davis, and Jonathan and Nathan Winship approached King Kamehameha. The King granted them a monopoly of Hawaii's sandalwood supply in exchange for one-fourth of the proceeds.

There were about seven species of sandalwood in the Hawaiian Islands. Sandalwood hit a commercial jackpot for King Kamehameha and his island kingdom.

After delivering a tidy profit to the King from the first sale to China interests, King Kamehameha granted the traders a 10-year-monopoly on the sandalwood harvest. The traders immediately sailed back to Canton with five shiploads of the wondrous wood, bringing another handsome profit.

The War of 1812 between Britain and the United States brought a halt to the shipments.

American ships were taking refuge in the Hawaiian Islands and Kamehameha refused to honor his contract with the traders. The traders blamed interference from the British for this cancellation.

After the war, the sandalwood trade again flourished and for fifteen years was the main source of revenue for the rulers of the Sandwich Islands.

Kamehameha decided to skirt the use of middlemen. He purchased the British ship *Forester*, and renamed it *Taamano* after his favorite queen, Kaahumanu. Kamehameha sent the ship loaded with sandalwood to Canton on February 17, 1817.

His inexperienced crew was fleeced right and left in dealing with the Chinese. The cost of the voyage left Kamehameha with a $3,000 deficit. The high costs were blamed on "port fees," which Kamehameha had never heard of. From the experience Kamehameha did learn a lesson.

Thereafter, foreign ships entering Honolulu would pay the king a harbor fee of $80, besides $12 for the services of John Harbottle, the port pilot. The King also traded in sandalwood thereafter on an f.o.b. basis.

The King placed a *kapu* on the harvest of sandalwood, keeping the commercial trading in this product strictly a royal monopoly. The coin in his royal treasury continued to grow and Kamehameha was able to add six ships to his fleet, all of them paid for with sandalwood.

As the value of sandalwood increased, the Hawaiian Islands emerged as a prime source of raw material. Hawaii soon became known as "Tahn Heung Sahn", the Sandalwood Mountains. A *picul*, a unit that equals the amount a man can carry, or 133 1/2 pounds, sold for eight dollars.

In the early years, American entrepreneurs dealt with the King and chiefs. King Kamehameha had an exclusive monopoly over the sandalwood trade. He accumulated large amounts of luxury goods, often paying inflated prices for them.

The common people were ordered by the King to go into the mountains to cut sandalwood and carry the *iliahi* harvest to the harbor. After the bark and sapwood had been adzed off, the men would tie the heavy wood bundles on their backs and carry it down trails to areas that were dug to the same dimensions as the hulls of the cargo ships that transported the sandalwood to China.

Sharing in the sandalwood wealth was King Kaumualii of Kauai. Kaumualii was very inept at the business of trade. He maintained delusions, as well, about his buying power.

As his traders took his orders for goods they would obtain in China, Kaumualii said, "I hear that other kings have jewels of great beauty, and I have none. What are these jewels?"

He was told there are various kinds of jewels, but that diamonds were the most precious.

"Then bring me back a diamond," Kaumualii said. The trader asked the king what size diamond he would like.

"Well, say one about the size of a coconut."

Men, women and children carried the wood down to the sea on their naked backs. As the trees became even less abundant, the burden on the laborers, forced to search ever higher in the mountains, grew worse. Some workers deliberately uprooted saplings to drive the tree to extinction and ensure that their children would not have to do the same cruel work.

By the end of the 1820s, the forests were almost entirely denuded, the traditional Hawaiian agricultural system had collapsed, and some chiefs found themselves greatly in debt to foreign merchants, with no obvious way to pay.

After 1830, the sandalwood trade collapsed. The quality had degenerated and reckless exploitation had shut off the supply.

Chapter 5

The Parker Ranch

Parker Ranch paniolos ready for work.

Cattle were over-running the Hawaiian hills and meadows decades before the cattle industry became established in the American West.

Captain George Vancouver brought longhorn cattle from Santa Barbara, California to Hawaii in 1793. The animals ran wild. They demolished forestland, and in some places, drove out the natives by trampling the unfenced taro patches and truck gardens.

Little use was made of the interior or semi-barren uplands on Hawaii Island before John Palmer Parker, an American, started a small ranch in Kohala. He built his herd by taming the wild cattle descended from Vancouver's gift to King Kamehameha.

Parker, born in Newton, Massachusetts in 1790, settled at Waimea, Hawaii in 1815. His job for the king was to shoot the wild cattle, prepare their hides, and salt the beef for sale to visiting ships.

Skillful management built the cattle business into the great Parker Ranch, the second largest ranch under the American flag. The King Ranch in Texas is the largest.

California vaqueros, the Spanish *paniolos*, were persuaded to come to Hawaii to teach the Hawaiians how to ride and rope. They brought with them their high-horned saddles and covered stirrups, braided *reatas* and long spurs.

Hawaiians quickly adapted to this dashing sport. The king owned all of the wild herds, and the right to slaughter was let out on contract. The king, in the early 1800's, met with 245 chiefs. Under a program known as the *Great Mahele*, he divided the land.

The lands that he kept for himself and his family were called crown lands. The divisions that he reserved for the government were known as government lands. The land that he gave to the chiefs to own forever was called the *konohiki* lands.

The king made separate arrangements with each chief. All these arrangements by the king were recorded in a book called the *Mahele* (division) book. It took many months to complete this process, but when finally complete, the division book was known as the *Great Mahele*.

This was a good start on reforming the land system. It meant the government now owned some land, and the government could now sell or barter its land and make some money. Just maybe, the government could sell land and pay off the national debt, and put some money into the school system.

The Great Mahele did not solve all of the land problems. Most of the people of Hawaii were not chiefs. Consequently, most of the people of Hawaii were still without any land of their own.

In the 1850s, Hawaii began importing breeding cattle, both Aberdeen Angus and Hereford. A Durham bull was imported in 1854 and Devon cattle in 1855.

It was estimated that there were as many as forty thousand head of cattle in Hawaii. As late as 1875, hides and tallow was worth more than the meat. About one-fourth of all land in the islands today is still pasture.

Many of the pastures in Hawaii were so waterless; the cows grew up there without ever getting a drink of water. The animals existed on the heavy dews that clung to the grass each morning.

Parker Ranch, on the Big Island of Hawaii, is one of the largest ranches in the United States and home of Hawaii's cowboy, or *paniolo*. Paniolos are a tough, hard-riding breed of cowboy that worked six generations at the Parker Ranch, which is comprised of approximately 175,000 acres, 250 horses and 30,000 to 35,000 head of cattle.

Samuel Parker, a grandson of John Parker, inherited large landed estates on Hawaii from his maternal grandmother and mother, who were Hawaiian chieftesses. Samuel was one of the most capable Hawaiians of mixed blood, and popular with both foreigners and natives.

Parker Ranch Foundation Trust now owns the Parker Ranch. Former owner Richard Palmer Smart created this trust when he died in 1992. The trust foundation was created exclusively for health care, education and charitable purposes.

Chapter 6

Chinese 'Coolie' Labor

Captain Cook saw fields of sugar cane fields planted by the Hawaiian natives when he accidentally discovered the islands.

Thomas Manby, too, who came to the islands with Captain George Vancouver, wrote about the lush growth of the sugar cane.

"The sugar cane grows to a prodigious size and is spontaneous in many places; they fatten their hogs on it, which gives the pork a very superior richness to any I ever tasted in Europe."

Sugar cane was one of the earliest crops grown in the Sandwich Islands that are now called Hawaii. A Chinese man, Wong Tze Chun, grew a small amount of sugar cane on Lanai as early as 1802. He processed it with a crude stone mill brought from his homeland.

There were reports of others growing the crop as well. An Italian named Lavinia produced sugar in 1823. He used natives to crush the cane on poi-boards and boiled the juice in a copper kettle. One of the main early uses for the crop was the making of rum.

Ladd & Company made the first extensive planting at Koloa, Kauai about 1835. The company received a 50-year lease on the land to get started. The company produced two tons of sugar in 1837 after a terrible start.

Four tons of sugar was exported in 1836, but that figure increased to 375 tons by 1850, and swelled to 9,586 tons by the end of the reign of King Kamehameha V.

Sugar's future did look bright indeed. Shortage of labor was the main drawback because the Hawaiian natives did not like to work very hard. They preferred to put their energies into projects that promised them immediate excitement rather than a foundation for their future.

The Royal Hawaiian Agricultural Society tackled the labor shortage problem in 1850. Hawaii's national legislature passed the Masters and Servants Act.

Under the Masters and Servants Act, immigrant workers from China seemed ideal. They were the hardest workers available and they did not demand high wages. They had little regard for low-class living conditions and clothing, which made them even more attractive to sugar plantation owners, and easier to maintain as plantation workers.

The *luna* was the overseer of the workers. This relationship was probably the single biggest contributor to strife and tension on the plantations. This stemmed from the fact that *lunas* were usually Hawaiian, German, Portuguese or Norwegian, which caused racial conflict, as other ethnicities, such as Chinese and Japanese, could not achieve such status.

The *luna* too often was someone who did not know the language or the cultural background of the Asian workers, let alone the extent of his agricultural knowledge and skills.

Under the Masters and Servants Act, laborers could come into Hawaii as five-year plantation apprentices. After Hawaii passed its servants act, some 200 Chinese men boarded the *Thetis* to become the first organized shipment here. They earned free passage, $3 a month, room and board—in exchange for a five-year labor contract.

As the penal clauses of the Masters and Servants Act were invoked, a number of recalcitrant coolies refused to work. These dissidents found themselves in the fort at Honolulu on bread and water. A few plantation owners used whips on the "coolie" labor and one shot a coolie in the leg.

When their contract was up, many Chinese merged into the Hawaiian community—and soon were accused of gambling, sex and crime, as well as bringing leprosy, smallpox and opium use to Hawaii. These were not the first Chinese brought to the islands. Captain George Vancouver, who brought cattle from California to Hawaii in 1794, remembered seeing a Chinese person at that time.

A Chinese man living on Lanai in 1802 was supposed to have been the first man in the kingdom to boil sugar, and during the next half-century a few Chinese started one-man sugar plantations and mills on the outer islands.

Between 1866 and 1884, Chinese in Hawaii grew from 1,200 to 18,000-plus. The lopsidedness of males to females spurred Hawaii's Cabinet Council in 1883 to restrict Chinese immigration to 2,400 per year. Tens of thousands of Chinese left over the next 20 years.

In these early years of Chinese immigration, most of the men from China came to earn money for their families at home. They had no intention of remaining in Hawaii beyond the term of their labor contracts. Approximately one-half of the early immigrants did return to China.

During this period, a small number of workers returned to China to bring their wives to Hawaii or sent for them. However, many of the Chinese men married Hawaiian women and settled in Hawaii.

As their plantation contracts ended, many Chinese left the plantations, choosing to pursue other means of survival. They became carpenters, farmed taro, planted rice and some established retail businesses. They formed clan societies, established temples, cemeteries, language schools, and Chinese newspapers to retain their cultural identity.

For many, Hawaii was no longer a temporary stopping place, but a permanent home. An 1851 census showed there were only 71 Chinese, 1962 foreigners from other lands, and 84,165 native Hawaiians.

The importation of Chinese was abruptly stopped in 1898 to avoid the establishment of an excessively large Chinese population. When Hawaii became a territory in 1900, Chinese labor was banned with some exceptions.

Chapter 7

The Hawaiian Goddess Pele

There are various versions of the legend about Pele, the Hawaiian queen of fire and the goddess of volcanoes. Pele was passionate, volatile and capricious. She is the most visible of all the gods and goddesses in Hawaiian history.

In her legend, Pele was the daughter of *Haumea*, a goddess of fertility and childbirth. She had five brothers and eight sisters. Her favorite residence was the vast and ever-seething crater of Kilauea on the Big Island of Hawaii, where she spewed ribbons of hot lava down the mountainside.

Pele once lived in *Kahiki*, a word meaning "out of sight" in Hawaiian. This might be interpreted as "over the horizon," "in outer space," or in "the spirit world". Pele longed to travel. She borrowed a canoe from a brother, and with some siblings, landed first at Lehua, a small volcanic cone sticking up out of the water north of Niihau.

One part of Pele's legend is that she was driven from her home by her sister *Na-maka-o-ka-ha'i* for seducing her husband.

Pele first landed on Kauai, but every time she thrust her *o'o* (digging stick) into the earth to dig a pit in which to live, Na-maka-o-ka-ha, goddess of water and the sea, would flood the pits. Pele

43

kept moving down the chain of islands in order of their formation. She eventually landed on the Big Island's Mauna Loa.

Here, legend notes that Na-maka-o-kaha'i could not send the ocean's waves high enough on Mauna Loa to drown Pele's fires, so Pele established her home on its slopes. From her home here, Pele welcomed her brothers.

A view of Kilauea's crater where the fabled Pele made her home.

(California State Library)

On a cliff nearby is Kilauea Mountain, which is sacred to her eldest brother, *Ka-moho-ali*. He is king of the sharks and the keeper of the gourd that held the water of life, which gave him the power to revive the dead.

Pele and two of her sisters, *Hi'iaka* and *Laka*, were all patronesses of the dance. Pele traveled in spirit form to the north shore of Kauai to witness a dance performance at a *pahula* or dance platform.

She manifested herself as a desirable young woman, and fell in love with the handsome young chief named *Lohi'au*. He did not suspect that Pele was a goddess and he fell madly in love with her.

They were wed, but soon after, Pele had to go back to her sleeping body in her volcano home on the Big Island. She promised to quickly return. Lohiau waited anxiously for her.

After a time Pele sent her favorite sister *Hi'iaka*, goddess of the sea, to fetch the prince. Hi'iaka and Lohiau took such a long time returning that Pele grew suspicious of them and tried to kill them both. Lohiau was killed, but Hi'iaka returned his spirit to his body.

Still other myths about Pele abound. One is that Pele would wander up to people while in the form of an old beggar woman. She would ask for food and drink. She punished those who were greedy and unkind to her by having their homes and crops destroyed. They, in turn, then had to rely on the kindness of others.

Unlike other gods and goddesses, no human sacrifices were ever made to Pele. For her, red berries were given in ancient times, but in later days, offerings included gin or brandy.

Pele was depicted as a wanderer. She constantly traveled through her domain. Pele sightings have been reported over the islands of

Hawaii for hundreds of years, but especially near her home, Mount Kilauea.

One interesting Pele legend says she was forced to go from island to island as she was chased by various other gods, most of them her relatives. The journey took her from the island of Kauai to the island of Hawaii, where she presently lives.

Her movements correspond with modern scientific notions about the age of the volcanoes.

Stories of Pele and her lovers abound. It is noteworthy that most of her lovers were not lucky enough to escape with their lives when she hurled molten lava at them.

One lover proved a match for Pele. This was *Kamapua'a*, a demi-god. This pig-god hid the bristles growing down his back with a cape. He and Pele were constantly at odds. She covered the land with barren lava, and he brought torrents of rain to extinguish her fires. He also called the wild boars to dig up the land, softening it so seeds could grow.

Pele and Kamapua'a raged against each other until her brothers begged her to give in. They feared that Kamapua'a's storms would soak all the fire sticks and kill Pele's power to restore fire.

The fire goddess has added seventy acres of land to Hawaii's coastline with her lava spewing ways.

Chapter 8

The Early Polynesians

The ancient Polynesians were part of a Stone Age culture. Their migration to Hawaii was one of the most remarkable achievements in history. This migration began before the birth of Christ.

When the Polynesians crossed the Pacific Ocean, they did so without compass or sextant. This feat was deemed impossible by the first Europeans to see the Polynesian settlements. The Europeans held to the belief that the Polynesians did not make the ocean crossing intentionally, but were blown off

This stone image from Necker Island in the Hawaiian archipelago is 3,000 miles from its counterpart in the Marquesas, yet looks very similar.

(Courtesy Jane Resture)

course or encountered currents that carried them accidentally to the new shores.

Making this trip by accident would be extremely difficult. Waves in the Pacific Ocean are as big as two-story buildings, and the distance between the Polynesian islands is vast. It is more than two thousand miles from Tahiti to Hawaii.

Europeans were sailing close to the coastlines of continents before navigational instruments were available, but they did not venture onto the open ocean.

This was not so with the explorers from Fiji, Tonga and Samoa. They began to settle islands in an ocean area of more than ten million square miles.

Making the voyaging across the open ocean more remarkable was that it was done in canoes built with tools of stone, bone, and coral. To navigate, these early-day sailors depended on their observations of the ocean and sky and traditional knowledge of the sea and winds.

Cracks and seams in the canoes were sealed with coconut fibers and sap from breadfruit or other trees. The canoes were paddled when there was no wind and sailed when there was enough breeze. The sails were woven from coconut or pandanus leaves.

Andia y Varela visited the Society Island in 1874. He took note of the canoes he saw: "It would give the most skilful [European] builder a shock to see craft having no more breadth of beam than three [arm] spans carrying a spread of sail so large as to befit one of ours with a beam of eight or ten spans..." Varela also seized on the fact that the canoe sailors had no means of lowering or furling the sail.

The Polynesian canoes were seaworthy and faster than the ships of the European explorers. An outrigger was attached to a single hull for greater stability on the ocean; two hulls were lashed together with crossbeams and a deck was added between the hulls for long voyages.

One of the most important tools of the Polynesian explorers was the "star compass". It isn't enough for the navigator to simply look up into the sky to get his bearings. He must be able to identify the stars and watch where they rise and set every night.

The task of the Polynesian sailors was especially difficult on cloudy days and nights. Under these conditions, the sailing master had only the course of the wind and the ocean swells on which to rely.

These sailing masters hit their destinations with as much precision as the most expert navigators of civilized nations could achieve.

Andia y Varela told of the methods of these early mariners in 1874. They have no mariner's compass, but divide the horizon into sixteen parts, taking for the cardinal points those at which the sun rises and sets.

When setting out from port the helmsman partitions the horizon, counting from E, or the point where the sun rises, said Varela. He thus knows when he sets out in which his destination bears.

Voyagers followed the flight of land-dwelling birds that fished at sea. The sailors took note as these birds flew from the direction of their islands in the morning and returned in the evening.

Researchers believe the people of Polynesia came from a common ancestral group that developed a distinctive fishing and farming culture in the islands of Tonga and Samoa.

Some scholars believe that early settlers of Hawaii came predominantly from the Marquesas. The close relationship between the Hawaiian and Marquesan languages offers strong corroborative evidence that the early Hawaiians came from the Marquesas.

Chapter 9

Bubonic Plague Strikes Honolulu

The burning of Chinatown halted bubonic plague epidemic in Honolulu. The same fire, however, started the downward spiral of the Chinese population in Hawaii. (Hawaii State Archives)

Honolulu was under quarantine, and the city's police force was stretched to its limits. The year was 1900.

Bubonic plague struck Honolulu and government officials vowed to do anything to save the city, including burning it to the ground.

Dockworkers on the *Pacific Mail* pier had the first inkling that something was wrong. Rats that scuttled around the pier behaved strangely. They would venture into the light and die in apparent agony.

Hundreds of rats soon littered the pier. Workers simply shrugged and swept the dead animals off into harbor water.

The Queen's Hospital noticed a significant upsurge in its patient admittals. In November, the hospital was so beleaguered it was forced to turn away a patient with tuberculosis. There had been

It was a fiery morning January 20, 1900, as embers burned Honolulu's Chinatown.
(Hawaii State Archives)

three mysterious deaths among the normally robust Hawaiian crew aboard the inter-island steamship Claudine.

52

One newspaper noticed that the death numbers for Hawaiians was triple that of white citizens. The Pacific Commercial Advertiser said, *"The complete disappearance of the race is only a question of time, and not a very long time at that."*

Doctors correctly diagnosed the disease. Fleas, sucking blood from infected rats, spread the "black plague" disease like a wild fire. The Board of Health in Honolulu sprang into action, even though Hawaii at the time had a caretaker government.

Members of the health board pored over reports of plague epidemics in China, Japan and India to gain an upper hand in fighting the disease. They, too, determined the bubonic plague disease came from infected rats.

Plague victims were moved to a temporary hospital outside of town. Passengers aboard ships were quarantined. The board established a quarantine district in Chinatown and posted guards there. A bevy of Japanese physicians presented themselves to the board for volunteer duty.

There were no crematories in Honolulu. Plague victims were burned in a spare furnace at Honolulu Iron Works. Within a few days, Iron Works employees built a crematorium on Quarantine Island (now known as Sand Island) to dispose of the dead.

Quarantine Island was a reeking sand bar surrounded by stagnant salt-water flats. The *Hawaiian Star* newspaper described it as "a wide swamp, filled with every kind of objectionable refuse, including the decaying bodies of animals."

The Board of Health set up an animal menagerie where it could test the effectiveness of the pathogen. Matter from plague victims was injected into animals. Some of them began dying within hours.

National Guard troops guarding the quarantine area pointed out to doctors that while people were locked inside the zone, their dogs and cats were running in and out of the quarantine area without restraint.

By December 14, of 1899, doctors began feeling some relief for their efforts. No new cases were being reported.

There was a rush on steamship offices to book passage away from the island. Board of Health president Henry Cooper issued an edict to ship captains that no one was to board or leave any ship, nor can cargo be taken on or off. If clean for seven days, the ships were allowed to sail. Even the mail arriving in Honolulu was fumigated.

The Board of Health lifted the Chinatown quarantine at noon, December 19, Board of Health offices was immediately swamped with applications to leave the islands. But it wasn't long until several reports of ill victims began resurfacing.

Dr. Cooper quickly scheduled a meeting of the Board of Health. It was determined that four specific streets surrounded the epicenter of contagion. It was decided to begin burning down homes and business where plague was suspected in an attempt to stop its rampage.

It was determined that buildings in the area would be posted and condemned on the spot. The people would only have time to get out, taking few of their belongings, before the buildings would be burned.

The National Guard ordered eighty-five Chinese people on Nuuanu Street out. The people were taken to an enclosed, locked shooting range in Kakaako where their belongings were doused with lime and hauled away.

By mid-afternoon, the Honolulu Fire Department wagons were in place and the Nuuanu structure was set ablaze.

The Chinese in Honolulu felt health authorities were unfairly targeting them. Although thousands of Hawaiian and Japanese were uprooted as well, it was Chinese-owned businesses that absorbed the brunt of property damage.

Chinese made up a considerable percentage of Honolulu's population. By the mid-1990s, one in five residents of Hawaii was of Chinese descent. Many Chinese had put down roots, established schools, newspapers, cemeteries, temples and clan societies.

Unlike other groups, however, the Chinese did not assimilate into Hawaiian culture. They preferred to form their own separate societies.

When Honolulu finally decided to build a sewer line through Chinatown in 1899, workers discovered they were digging through compacted layers of fermenting garbage.

With the onset of the "Black Death," health inspectors made quick field trips into Chinatown. They came back horrified. The district was full of reeking outdoor toilets and backyard cesspools.

The area was swarming with rats, maggots, flies, lice and cockroaches.

The only solution was to burn Chinatown down. Because of the possible indictment of Honolulu police from public opinion over such a burning, it was decided to let the military do it. Within hours, all Honolulu police were withdrawn from the quarantine zone. Although martial law had not been declared, soldiers were allowed to proceed as though it had.

A committee of businessmen was formed to find warehouse space for goods removed from Chinatown stores that were being burned. During the first three weeks of January 1900, buildings were torched nearly every day.

Deaths from the plague still kept happening. Then five plague deaths were reported at Nuuanu and Beretania streets, making this area a hotspot for pestilence. Officials decided to burn the entire area on January 20.

Most of the firemen in Honolulu were on the scene, but about an hour after the fire was lit, a strong wind scattered embers across neighboring rooftops. Flying embers were sent unchecked onto the wooden buildings of Chinatown.

Fire spread out blocks away from the original fire. As firemen attempted to save a burning church, the side of the building exploded, slamming a whirlwind of fiery debris into the fire engine. The fire horses bolted and by the time the nervous creatures were caught; the fire engine had been consumed.

Building after building began to ignite throughout the area. *The Hawaiian Star* reported simply, "Chinatown is wiped out."

As city officials struggled to cope with the many homeless brought on as a result of the fire, there was one positive note. There was only one new case of the plague reported that day.

Hawaii's Chinese population never recovered from the devastating fire. The numbers of Chinese in Hawaii dropped from twenty percent of its population to less than five percent in the 1990 census.

Some good did come of the fire. Honolulu officials began a frenzy of sewer building and other sanitation-oriented public works. It was never known exactly how many deaths resulted from bubonic plague. It is known that no deaths resulted from the massive Chinatown fire.

Chapter 10

Pineapple Comes to Hawaii

The pineapple industry began as a struggling supplement to the sugar industry late in the nineteenth century.

Don Francisco de Paula Marin served as interpreter and trusted advisor to Kamehameha

I. He was made a chief by Kamehameha and given some tracts of land. He is believed responsible for introducing the pineapple to Hawaii.

Known as "Minini" to the Hawaiians, Marin cultivated large stretches of garden land and pasture and introduced dozens of useful plants into the islands. Most of the early plant wealth of

This is the only known image of Don Francisco de Paula Marin and is taken from an engraving made in 1837.

the islands derived from seeds, roots, and cuttings introduced by Marin.

59

Marin was a one-man agricultural experiment station. From friends in Spanish America, he obtained plants to supplement the native flora, and successfully adapted them to Hawaiian soil.

Early in his island residency, Marin cultivated pineapples, oranges, grapes, peaches, cherimoyas, melons, figs, lemons, beans, cabbages, potatoes, horseradish, carrots, asparagus, corn, lettuce, roses, and tobacco. Later he grew coffee, cotton, clover, tomatoes, turnips, peppers, wheat, and barley.

Marin experimented also in making coconut oil, candlenut oil, castor oil, soap, sugar, molasses, pickles, and lemon syrup.

He manufactured lime, tiles, hay, nails, cigars, candles, beer, wine and brandy.

Missionary Laura Fish Judd duly noted that Marin was very selfish about his plants. When he trimmed his vines and roses he would burn the trimmings instead of distributing them among others.

The missionary wrote, "When we arrived at Honolulu, in 1826, there was not a vine or fig tree to be found outside of his garden, except a few obtained from other sources."

Marin later owned Ford Island on Oahu, and raised hogs, goats, and rabbits. Some say he once owned nearly all of the cattle on Oahu, as well as a number of horses, sheep, and extensive tracts of land.

Most of the plants collected by Marin failed to thrive in Hawaii, but it is suspected that some of the plant pests now found in Hawaii might have come in with Marin's introductions.

American Factors was among the top five in the sugar industry, along with Castle and Cooke, Alexander and Baldwin, Theo. Davis & Co., and C. Brewer & Co.

Pineapple developed as a promising second staple for the islands. It supplied three fourths of the world market.

It was important enough that James Dole, head of the Hawaiian Pineapple Company, bought the entire island of Lanai in 1922 to grow pineapple. Dole paid a little more than one million dollars for the island, and his company then led the industry.

When Hawaii was annexed to the United States, the U.S. was fearful that Hawaii would put all of its eggs into one "sugar" basket. The U.S. Department of Agriculture established an experiment station on the outskirts of Honolulu in 1901.

The thrust of research for the new station was to seek new crops and industry for Hawaii. The work of the experiment station contributed materially to the successful establishment of the pineapple industry.

By the end of the 19th century, sugar and pineapple plantations run by American businessmen had overtaken much of Hawaii's land and the crops were the two most important sources of revenue for the Hawaiian economy.

Pineapple harvest at Maui Pineapple Company.

Even though the pineapple industry was on its way to becoming a new industry for Hawaii, it had a mineral problem in its soil It was the experiment station that developed an iron sulfate treatment that enabled the industry to occupy large land areas on which it could not previously grow because of high manganese content in the soil.

Don Francisco de Paula Marin would be proud of what has become of his early introduction of the pineapple.

Chapter 11

Father Damien Among the Lepers

Father Damien
(Google Images)

L eprosy came to Hawaii during the reign of Kamehameha III. It is believed to have come from China, a belief supported by the common Hawaiian name for leprosy, *Mai Pake* (Chinese disease)

Other references say a native chief that had traveled abroad about 1840 brought the disease back to Hawaii.

Leprosy had been observed in the kingdom as early as 1830. The Norwegian scientist Armauer Hansen identified the *bacillus leprae* in 1868.

63

Many white men on the islands shared the widespread belief that leprosy was associated with venereal disease, perhaps even a form of it. It was not surprising to them that leprosy found most of its victims among the natives.

Little was done to curb the spread of leprosy during its early years. By the beginning of the reign of Kamehameha V, it was so noticeable that it created considerable alarm.

Kamehameha addressed the legislature in October 1864. He convinced the body that something had to be done to stop the spread of the disease. The legislature approved setting aside a small peninsula on the north side of Molokai for a leper settlement.

The natives opposed this policy. They did not fear the disease nor felt a necessity for such a vigorous assault. Also, they did not want prying officials inspecting their living.

One man, a native of Kauai named Koolau, refused to go to Molokai. He fled with his family and a small group of diseased Hawaiians into the almost inaccessible valley of Kalalau, and for months, he stood off the law with his rifle. He killed several deputies and outlasted the sheriff's posses. He died a free man, but still a leper, and because he was a leper, he died a murderer.

Lepers who were considered incurable were isolated at Molokai. By the end of Kamehameha's reign, about eight hundred lepers were sent to the Molokai settlement. Nearly all were native Hawaiians.

Joseph De Veuster, from Belgium, arrived in Honolulu on March 19, 1864. There he was ordained in the Cathedral of Our Lady of Peace, and took the name Damien. He spent eight years serving his faith on the big island of Hawaii.

He then learned of the desperate need for priests to serve the several hundred Hansen's disease victims quarantined at Molokai in the leper community of Kalawao. With his arrival, Kalawao became a place to live rather than to die.

There was a reason for people with the disease to feel desperate. It was an incurable disease.

Father Damien offered hope to the victims of the dread disease. He spoke to them in their native Hawaiian language. He encouraged the patients to build houses, construct a water system, and plant trees. Under his tutelage, schools were organized, and included bands and choirs.

It was found that children born into the leper colony did not inherit the disease. One man on Molokai married in succession two leprous women, both of who died, and both bore seemingly healthy children. With the consent of the parents, these "clean" children were removed from the colony and reared in private families, or in the case of girls, in the Kapiolani Home, under the care of the Franciscan Sisters.

At one point, the leper segregation and treatment program was allowed to break down. Lepers were allowed to buy exemptions to escape being sent to the colony on Molokai.

Damien badgered the Hawaiian government for more resources, and his efforts soon attracted worldwide attention. Others came to help Father Damien minister to the afflicted.

By the end of the 1870s, more than a thousands lepers were sent to Molokai, isolated from all their friends, family, and the other islands. It was feared at one time the disease might completely wipe out the Hawaiian race.

Father Damien lived in Kalawao for twelve years when he, too, fell victim to leprosy. He had been lax about his hygiene in regard to the disease. Damien dipped his fingers in the poi bowl along with the patients. He shared his pipe with them. And he did not always wash his hands after bandaging open sores.

Chapter 12

The Royal Hawaiian Band

The Royal Hawaiian Band was first organized in 1870 as a government institution. Bandleader is Aaron Mahi. (California State Library)

T he Royal Hawaiian Band was founded by Kamehameha III in 1836, and remains one of the active links to the monarchy.

This musical group remains a vital part of Hawaii's daily life as the islands changed from a monarchy to a territory and finally to become the 50th State of the United States.

The Royal Hawaiian Band has the distinction of being the first brass band in the Pacific, the second oldest community band and the only full-time municipal band in the United States.

In 1848, Wilhelm Merseburgh from Weimar assumed leadership of the Royal Hawaiian Band. Merseburgh was indicative of a growing European presence in Hawaii during the 19th century.

King Kamehameha V requested the services of the Prussian government to update Hawaii's national band. This brought Heinrich "Henry" Berger of Potsdam to Honolulu.

Berger was loaned to Hawaii by the imperial German government in 1872, but he became a naturalized Hawaiian subject in1879.

Berger was so well accepted by the Hawaiians that he served as bandmaster for 43 years. He directed the Royal Hawaiian Band in more than 32,000 concerts, arranged more than 1,000 western and 200 Hawaiian melodies. Berger penned 600 compositions, many of which became Hawaii's best-loved songs, including one that became Hawaii's national anthem.

Mekia Kealaka`i (1867-1944) is one of the band's most noted accomplishments. Mekia ("major" in Hawaiian), so named because his father was a sergeant major, emerged from poverty to become one of the most respected musicians of his day, as an instrumentalist, composer, troubadour and finally as the bandmaster of the Royal Hawaiian Band.

His musical training began in reform school, where he was sent at age 12 for truancy. Captain Henry Berger taught music there, and the boys who showed talent were recruited into the Royal Hawaiian Band. Mekia Kealaka`i was one of these. He spent many hours learning harmony and how to play trombone, flute and piano, and became one of Berger's favored pupils.

Although he was admitted into the band as a trombonist, it was Mekia's flute playing on a US mainland tour in 1895 that so impressed John Philip Sousa, that Mekia was invited to join Sousa's band.

The March King once remarked that Mekia was "the greatest flutist I have ever heard." For more than 20 years Kealaka`i toured the US and Europe; his three years in London performing at the Palladium, Savoy and Crystal Palace helped to spark the interest in Hawaiian music which still exists in England.

Mayor John H. Wilson called Mekia Kealaka`i back to Honolulu in 1920 to lead the Royal Hawaiian Band because "Hawaii needs you to help preserve her music." Under Mekia's strong leadership, the band kept its Hawaiian character, Hawaiian membership and emphasis on Hawaiian songs. From reform school to Bandmaster, he served for 40 years in the Royal Hawaiian Band.

The Royal Hawaiian Band is made up of 40 full-time positions. It functions as a concert band, a marching band and a glee-club ensemble.

Weekly concerts hold forth at the Iolani Palace grounds. These are among the 305-plus shows the band plays each year. Its vast array of music express the various forms of musical styles found in Hawaii.

Today, the Royal Hawaiian Band is an agency of the City and County of Honolulu. The band has traveled extensively since its inception, performing in the mainland United States, Canada, Europe and Japan. The band performed a historic concert to a packed house in New York City's Carnegie Hall.

Chapter 13

Breaking Hawaii's Kapu System

Hawaii's *kapu* (taboo) was a complicated device to perpetuate the prestige and power of the priests. There were *kapu* for everything from building a house to making tools or weapons. *Alii* (chiefs) and *kahuna's* (priests) handed down the laws, rituals and rules (*kapu*).

Kukailimoku, Hawaiian God of War
(Bishop Museum)

The system came to an end in a dramatic highly symbolic event in 1819.

One kapu was that women must eat separately from men, and eat a different diet.

Commoners had to lie down on the ground when *alii* approached. The penalties were severe, often death, and quickly meted out by the *mu*. The *mu* was the person who procured men for sacrifice in Hawaiian rituals.

One example, if two young girls were seen eating a banana, which was

71

forbidden fruit for women, their immediate guardian was quickly put to death. Another child had her eye scooped out for daring to taste a banana.

Because the early Hawaiians depended on nature for everything, the *kapu* system was intimately connected with reverence and respect for the natural world. This *Aloha Aina* (love of the land) made the *kapu* system one of the earliest examples of environmental protection.

The *kapu* system separated Hawaiian society into four groups of people:

- The *alii*, or chiefs, ruled specific territories and held their positions on the basis of family ties and leadership abilities. The chiefs were thought to be descendants of the gods and the highest chiefs, *alii,* were considered gods;
- The *kahuna* were priests or skilled craftspersons. They performed important religious ceremonies and served the *alii* as close advisers;
- The *makaainana*, were commoners (by far the largest group) who raised, stored, and prepared food, built houses and canoes, and performed other daily tasks;
- The *kauwa*, (outcasts), were forced to lead lives segregated from the rest of Hawaiian society.

There were different *kapu* for different infractions. The most serious were laws of the gods, *kapu akua*, and laws of the chief, *kapu alii*.

The chief had power over life and death. All he had to do was utter the word and a person would be killed.

The chief could also utter a word to spare a life. As formidable as some *kapu* were there was also a *kapu akua* (a law of the gods) providing for pardon, clemency, absolution, and mercy. This was known as *puuhonua* or "refuge" from capital punishment.

When King Kamehameha I died, his son Liholiho assumed the throne. Liholiho took the name Kamehameha II.

He was not a strong ruler, and easily influenced by the opinions of his mother and his aunt, Queen Kaahumanu, both of who objected to the *kapu* against their sex, particularly at eating time.

The women convinced Liholiho to conduct an experiment. King Kamehameha II invited all the leading chiefs and foreigners on the island to a feast. Two tables were set, European fashion, one for the men and one for the women.

After everyone started to eat, the king moved about the tables. He suddenly took a seat at the women's table, and nervously began to eat. Everyone could see he was not affected by the affront to the gods for violating *kapu*.

The astonished guests cried out, "The eating *kapu* is broken."

Liholiho was quick to remove other *kapu*. He issued an order to destroy the temples and the idols. Strangely, the high priest obeyed. However, many idols were hidden and some of the old beliefs lingered secretly. The king gave orders that men and women should eat together throughout the country and that no foods should be *kapu* to either.

When the priests and chiefs learned about the king's eating at the same table as the women without punishment, they were forced to admit that their religion was wrong, that the gods did not really exist. Hawaii thus became a nation and society that was godless, in a manner of speaking.

Six months later, the first Christian missionaries arrived in Hawaii and religion began its spread throughout the islands.

Kapu System

In 1782, King Kamehameha I chose to enforce early religious practices. These included many taboos about eating, especially directed at women, who in many societies are considered unclean.

As a result, "Males performed virtually all the work of food acquisition, cultivation and preparation. This meant the women were removed from the enjoyment of those foods they most prized."

While they ate from separate dishes in distanced eating houses, they were forbidden to eat pig, bananas, coconuts, turtle, the meat of the niuhi shark, the whale, the porpoise or the stingray.

The kapu system continued for forty years until the 1820's. Even today in the islands, it is Hawaiian men who are reckoned to be the better cooks."

Chapter 14

Kamehameha I Unites Hawaii

Kamehameha was born at Kohala, Hawaii. The year is uncertain but believed to about 1758, the year Halley's Comet passed over the Earth's skies.

At the time of his birth, a priest told his grandfather chief Alapainui that a rebel infant would be born to slay the chief. This prompted the chief to order all infants be killed at once.

Consequently, as soon as Kamehameha was delivered, the babe was spirited away to protect him from execution. Hawaiians believed that the birth of Kamehameha fulfilled their

Bronze Kamehameha Statue by Thomas R. Gould, Given in 1969; located in National Statuary Hall.

prophecy of a birth of a male who would vanquish all other chiefs in Hawaii.

Kamehameha was raised in seclusion for five years. He was then returned to the court of the king where he was brought up in royal custom. Little is known of his youth, but it is believed Kekuhaupio, one of the famous warriors at that time, instructed him in the arts of war.

At the time that Captain James Cook discovered Hawaii, the king of the island of Hawaii was Kalaniopuu, an uncle to Kamehameha. When the king became ill two years later, he attempted to provide for a peaceful succession by making it clear he wanted his elder son, Kiwalao, to be the next ruler.

Keowa, the younger brother, was a warlike and ambitious young man. His father gave him large estates. Kamehameha was given the post of custodian of the ancestral war god.

A series of quarrels began as soon as the old king died. Keowa attacked Kamehameha, and Kiwalao was drawn into the conflict. When the battle was over, the ruler of the island, Kiwalao, was dead. Keowa had fled, and Kamehameha had triumphed.

Kamehameha was ambitious. He invaded Maui with a great army, followed by eight hundred chiefs resplendent in feather cloaks and helmets, all led by the image of the war god, Kukailimoku.

In addition to clubs and spears some of the king's soldiers were armed with muskets and a small brass cannon, furnished by an American trader. With excellent strategy, Kamehameha recorded another victory.

After Maui was overrun, he moved on to Molokai, where Kahekili, his chief rival was living. Kamehameha sent a message to the old ruler offering war or peace. Kahekili refused to make a choice, but said that after his death, Kamehameha could take possession of his domain.

Kamehameha was unable to continue his negotiations with Kahekili. He had to return to Hawaii, where Keowa was again challenging his authority. During the fighting there, Kilauea volcano erupted, sending out stones, smoke and suffocating gas which enveloped Keowa's troops. Four hundred troops were killed.

This signaled the natives that the powerful goddess of volcanoes, Pele, was on the side of the king. Kamehameha celebrated his success by building a great temple to the war god.

Kahekili and his supporters again stirred up trouble by invading Hawaii with a large fleet. Kamehameha met them head on and defeated them.

By 1795, Kamehameha was ruler of all the islands except Kauai and Niihau. Twelve years later, he added them to his domain by negotiation.

Kamehameha had twenty-one wives, but his favorite was Kaahumanu, who he married when was only thirteen years old. She was described as handsome, and built on the grand Hawaiian scale. She was six feet tall and weighed two hundred pounds.

Throughout his life, Kamehameha maintained the ancient religion of the Hawaiians with great strictness. As official guardian of the war god that had brought him success in battle, he performed the necessary acts of worship.

The kapu system was observed, and as late as 1817, several persons were executed for violations of these religious bans. No missionaries of Christianity arrived in Hawaii during his lifetime.

Chapter 15

Statehood for Hawaii

The Hawaiian Flag

Statehood was proposed for Hawaii long before it ever became a state. The issue was first addressed in 1849 by a newspaper in New York State, which advocated annexation of the Hawaiian Islands and their admission into the union as the State of Hawaii.

John L. Stevens, American Minister to Hawaii, in 1893 tried to prod the U.S. into action. "The Hawaiian pear is now fully ripe, and this is the golden hour to pluck it," Stevens wrote.

The Democrats were generally opposed to annexation, while the Republicans favored it.

William McKinley was inaugurated as president June 16, 1897. Soon after, a new treaty of annexation was signed. The treaty was submitted to the U.S. Senate the same day. Opponents of the treaty fought hard to prevent its approval. While a majority of the senators were in favor of it, passage required a two-thirds vote.

While the U.S. Senate took no action in Washington, the treaty was approved in Hawaii by the Hawaiian Senate and signed by territorial President Dole.

The treaty was still pending in the U.S. when war broke out between the United States and Spain. Admiral Dewey destroyed the Spanish fleet in the Philippines and took possession of Manila Bay. U.S. troops were ordered to sail from San Francisco to Manila.

Instead of remaining neutral in this conflict, Hawaii offered the United States the use of its harbors and facilities. Troop ships were welcomed with enthusiasm. The value of the Hawaiian Island for military and naval purposes became perfectly clear, strengthening the cause of annexation.

When the U.S. Senate still took no action on the pending treaty, a different tact was used. This ploy involved the use of a resolution of the two houses of Congress, the same method used to bring about the annexation of Texas in 1845.

The joint resolution required only a majority vote of each house. It was passed by the House of Representatives on June 15, 1898, by the Senate on July 6, 1898, and signed by President McKinley the following day.

Chapter 16

The Whaling Industry in Hawaii

A whaling scene off the island of Hawaii in 1833.
(State Street Trust Company, Boston)

The whaling era in Hawaii lasted for about sixty years (1820-1880).

There was a great demand for whale oil and for whalebone. Articles that are now made from steel, celluloid, or rubber, were made out of whalebone in the 1880s. Whale oil was used in lamps and in the manufacture of candles, the chief source of artificial light.

Hundreds of whaling vessels scoured the seas in search of whales. In the first two decades of the

81

whaling trade, Honolulu was the only port that satisfied both shipmasters and common seamen.

The port city afforded good facilities for picking up supplies, and at the same time provided a place where sailors could be sure of finding liquor and women. At Lahaina on Maui, supplies were plentiful but the government refused to issue liquor licenses, so only staunch Christian whaling captains stopped there.

Two things happened to change this situation. First, Maui farmers began growing the white potato, and the sailors liked it much better than the sweet potato offered on Oahu. Secondly, Governor Hoapili of Maui died and the governors that followed allowed both grog shops and brothels to flourish.

The combination lure of the white potato and the prostitute resulted in twice as many whaling ships putting in at Lahaina than at Honolulu. During the mid-fifties, the potato boom died away and Honolulu again became an attraction for the whalers.

There is one story about a Japanese diplomatic mission stopping in Honolulu on its way to the U.S. Yanagawa Masakiyo, a member of the mission, wrote about a sightseeing walk the diplomats took.

"After we had walked about half a mile we saw a large house. There were many musical instruments in it. Several people were playing Hawaiian guitar, violin and castanet. We stood outside and listened because it was most interesting. One westerner came and led us upstairs. There we saw several hundred men and women in a large room, which was about 100 feet by 50 feet.

"A game of billiards was under way. When the ball went into the hole, a music box played automatically. This was a signal that the game had been won, so the lawyers drank wine and became very merry.

"We went upstairs and turned to the left, where we entered another long hall in which the light was very dim because of the scarcity of lamps. In this part of the building were about forty bedrooms. We thought this very strange and upon inquiry found it a house of ill fame. After the evening entertainment many of the guests retired to these rooms for which they paid $1.50 each."

Since the 1820s, whaling ships put in at Honolulu, Lahaina and lesser ports such as Hilo and Kealakekua on Hawaii, and at Waimea and Koloa on Kauai. In 1824, more than one hundred whalers used Hawaiian ports. In 1829, more than one hundred seventy moored in Hawaiian ports.

The Hawaiian Islands became the center of a booming trade. All this meant money, and not all went to the Hawaiian women waiting to service the sailors. The wages of native seamen, profits on the sale of supplies, commissions on the transshipments of oil and bone from the islands to the United States, made whaling indispensable to the island commerce.

The native constables made hay as well. They were given a percentage of fines imposed by the police courts. They would wait for a whaling ship to arrive, watch the liberty party hire horses, and then, as the seamen set off at a gallop, bring them to a stop and cite them for "furious riding."

The whaling industry in Hawaii reached its turning point about 1852. Thereafter, an ebb tide set in and the industry pretty much died by 1860.

Chapter 17

Coffee Is Hawaiian Staple

Ripening coffee beans
(Maui Coffee Co.)

C offee was introduced to Hawaii by Don Francisco de Paula Marin during the reign of Kamehameha I. Since that time, it has grown to be a staple agricultural crop for Hawaii.

The first planting that had any chance of success as a commercial venture was that of John Wilkinson, who came to Hawaii from England with Lord Byron, aboard the British warship H.M.S. *Blonde*. Also on board the *H.M.S. Blonde* were the bodies of King Kamehameha II and Queen Kamamalu, both of whom died in London from measles during a state visit.

Chief Boki, governor of Oahu, had encouraged Wilkinson to come and begin a plantation. Boki was in charge of the funeral party and had acquired coffee plants in Rio de Janeiro during the long voyage.

This vessel made a stop at Maui in 1800s to take on coffee and other products.
(Hawaii Historical Society)

He promised to help Wilkinson establish a plantation at Manoa Valley near Honolulu. Wilkinson encountered countless difficulties when he began planting in 1825. Tools were lacking, and the ground had to be broken up with the *o-o*, or digger, used by the natives.

Wilkinson soon found that native labor, at the rate of twenty-five cents per day, ate up a large portion of his capital. Before his project could bear fruit, in the spring of 1827, Wilkinson died, two years after the project began.

At the time of his death, he did have more than one hundred acres of sugar cane and a considerable number of coffee trees in the ground. Governor Boki and some of the foreign residents of Honolulu then took charge of the plantation.

The enterprise proved unprofitable, even though some molasses, sugar, and rum was produced from the sugar cane, and small amounts of sugar beans were picked by the natives.

Some plants were brought from Manila by the British Consul Richard Charlton and also set out in Manoa Valley.

In 1828, Reverend Samuel Ruggles planted coffee trees from the Manoa plantation in the Naole area above Kealakekua Bay on the Kona Coast. The plants thrived in this environment, due to the elevation, rich soil, and consistent cloud cover.

Missionaries began growing coffee in Hilo and Kona about 1828. From there, it was taken to Kauai in 1842 where a plantation was started at Hanalei. It was on Kauai that the first large coffee plantations were founded. A large area was planted at Hanalei in 1842, and another started in 1847.

The first record of coffee exportation was 248 pounds in 1845. In 1850, there were 208,428 pounds exported. The export amounts varied considerably during the early years. Floods, labor troubles and a severe drought blasted early prospects of success. Blight then hit the coffee industry in Kauai and caused growing of the product to be abandoned.

Hawaii's main outlet for coffee was the whaling industry. In the 1860's, the collapse of the whaling industry destroyed the primary market for Hawaiian coffee.

For several years after the overthrow of the monarchy, Hawaii's government offered coffee lands in an ultimately unsuccessful effort to draw Occidental farmers as settlers. Caucasian landholders dominated the plantation culture of coffee in Hawaii.

As coffee growing faltered, landowners in Kona divided their property into five-acre plots and took on tenants. Many of these were Japanese who had been plantation employees. The Japanese family predominance in coffee growing has lasted into a third generation.

At one time, as an incentive to encourage the growth of coffee plantings, Hawaii's successive governments would accept coffee as tax-payment tender. Additional encouragements were exemption from tariffs on imported mill equipment, tariff protection for local coffee, provision of public lands for lease, and land tax vacations.

During the 1930s, Hawaii earned a reputation for being a world leader in improving coffee cultivation methods. This has allowed Kona to maintain its reputation as one of the world's finest coffees.

Chapter 18

Japanese Immigrants in Hawaii

Japanese immigrant in Hawaii with his new "picture bride".

In the early nineteenth century the Hawaiian sugar cane industry had a relentless demand for labor, and to qualify, it had to be cheap labor.

Hawaiian natives had little desire to labor as plantation workers. The shortage of natives for the work force was compounded by Hawaiian emigration to the United States during the gold rush.

Chinese workers were imported in 1828, but the Chinese were quick to leave the plantations and set up their own enterprises in Hawaii, or else to return to China.

This led to the importation in 1868 of 148 Japanese immigrants, followed with another large cadre of Japanese workers in 1885. The importation of Japanese laborers caused concern for the Japanese government, which insisted on humanitarian safeguards about the treatment and rights of these workers.

The Japanese government's concern was justified, as the work was harsh and the workers were physically and orally abused by the plantation owners and overseers. When they did not understand orders given in English, workers were sometimes bullwhipped. The abuse grew so great that the workers complained to the Japanese government.

In response, Japan sent an ambassador to Hawaii to look into the problem. Fearing it would lose this important labor force, the Hawaiian government entered into an agreement with Japan making Japanese immigrants wards of the Hawaiian government.

Until it was sure that worker abuse was indeed stopped, Japan did not allow further emigration until 1886.

The Japanese staged the nation's first labor strike in 1891. When the sugar industry expanded, thousands of immigrants came to Hawaii under the contract system. Because some contracts were unfair, there were many complaints from the workers.

King Kalakaua tried his best to give the employees a better environment to work in. The first trade union started in 1884. After the annexation of Hawaii to the United States, contract labor was prohibited.

From the earliest days of Hawaii's sugar era, roughly in the mid-1850s, foreign workers began coming to the Hawaiian Islands in great numbers. The early *malahini,* or newcomers, came to work in the cane fields and mills.

They arrived in waves from around the globe as growers scoured the world for cheap and willing workers for their fields. In the early days these disparate strangers included Chinese, Filipinos, Japanese, Koreans, Portuguese and Puerto Ricans.

They were mostly housed, rent-free, in plantation camps spread around the island in close proximity to one of the nearly 20 mills and growing plantations, which dotted the landscape from Hana to Wailuku, and Ulupalakua to Lahaina.

With the plantation philosophy firmly in place, the owners housed their imported laborers in camps, usually segregated or with other distinguishing characteristics.

Some took on the names of older Hawaiian villages such as *Puunene* and *Paia.* Spanish Camp housed Puerto Ricans and Portuguese, Hawaiian Camp was home to native Hawaiians, and *Nashiwa Camp* was for Japanese.

While working conditions improved on many of the sugar cane plantations, the overwhelming trend was for the Japanese workers to leave at the earliest opportunity.

Most of the Japanese had two common plans when they came to Hawaii, One was to return home rich and triumphant, and the second was to make a home in the new land and achieve comfort and security.

Chapter 19

Incest, Infanticide and Polygamy

Hawaiian babies, especially girls, were routinely killed when parents didn't want to be bothered with raising them.

Infanticide was fearfully prevalent and most all of the older women at the time idolatry was abolished were guilty of it.

Historians repeatedly refer to the fact that as many as two-thirds of all children born in Hawaii when chiefs reigned supreme and commoners had little if any future, were simply put to death. Babies were most often buried alive to be rid of them, sometimes in the same house in which the parents lived.

On all the islands, the number of males was much greater than the number of females, a consequence of the fact that more infant daughters were subjected to infanticide than were the sons.

Sometimes, infants and children were given to others who wanted them. No regular parental discipline was practiced and the children were too often left to follow their own inclinations, and become familiar with the lowest vices.

The missionaries found it difficult to understand the Hawaiians. To them, when compared to New England standards, the islander's style of life was unhealthy and sluggish. Hawaiian women, particularly, thought hard work was a "disgrace".

Parents and friends arranged many marital engagements, generally on the side of the woman. There was not much of a marriage ceremony. Sometimes the groom would throw a piece of *Kapa* about the bride or friends would throw a piece over both the bride and the groom. Sometimes a feast would celebrate the marriage.

Missionaries disapproved of the leisurely life practiced by most Hawaiians.
(Hawaii Historical Society)

Under the pagan standards of the Hawaiians, it seemed there was not much natural affection among them. This seems to be supported by the fact that the marriage tenure was very uncertain, depending largely on the will of the husband.

When chiefs of high rank were married, they came in state with their attendants and joined noses before the assembly. The assembly would then shout *hoao na'lii e!* "...the chiefs are married!"

The first Christian marriage was not performed in Hawaii until August 11, 1822. The missionaries encountered great difficulty in imposing on the Hawaiians the same standards of sexual morality prevalent in New England.

The marriage tie was loose, and the husband could dismiss his wife without ceremony. Polygamy was allowed in all ranks, but practiced mostly by the chiefs who could best afford it.

An important step in popularizing the Christian ideal of marriage was taken in October 1823 when missionary William Richards united two powerful chiefs—Hoapili and Kalakua—in marriage.

Old age was generally despised among the commoners. The sick and those who had become helpless from age were sometimes abandoned to die or were put to death. Insane people were sometimes stoned to death.

Chapter 20

Hawaii Cotton Experience

A Hawaiian Cotton Plant

In the heady days of the mid-1800s, cotton made a brief attempt to vie with sugarcane as Hawaii's chief cash crop.

Some believe Hawaii cotton was a native plant of the Islands before the first Polynesian and Micronesian explorers and settlers arrived.

There truly is no native plant on Hawaii, as it was built up over years and years from volcanic lava spewing into the sea to the point the giant mountain ridge that is now Hawaii, was formed. Every bit of Hawaii's vegetation, animals and other resources came from someplace else.

Many plants now in Hawaii were borne there by birds, winds, ocean currents, or by people who began to inhabit the islands some 2,000 years ago.

Farmers were cultivating wild Hawaiian cotton as early as 1815, usually on small subsistence plots. Natives were raising cotton of excellent quality in 1825. The cotton fiber was so good that missionaries asked their governing board in New England to send someone to teach spinning and weaving.

The board sent Miss Lydia Brown to teach the art to the island natives. The young native women quickly caught onto the spinning technique, but it was the young men that were more adept at working the loom.

Hawaii's then Governor Kuakini decided to help the enterprise along. He instructed that a stone building be erected at Kailua to be used as a cotton factory.

When Hawaii's big farmers became more intensely interested in the crop as a commercial venture, they preferred the sea island variety they obtained from the Carolinas and Georgia on the U.S. mainland.

Called *ma'o* in the Hawaiian language, some thought Hawaiian cotton was of superior fiber and better adapted to the Hawaiian climate. Mainland planters, however, downgraded Hawaiian cotton primarily because it was an unknown, and because it was Hawaiian. There was widespread thinking that "All things Hawaiian were inferior."

Kamehameha III (1813-1854) was persuaded to give up royal ownership of all the lands in the *Great Mahele* (land division) of 1848. This would allow both Hawaiians and foreigners to buy and own land.

Almost from the beginning, the interests of the chiefs and the interests of white men were in conflict. The issue grew more combative each year. The issue would have to be resolved, and if the islands were ever to live up to their potential as an outpost of civilization in the Pacific, it would have be resolved the white man's way.

This allowed non-native Hawaiian entrepreneurs to amass huge tracts of land and begin looking for crops to grow. Many of these entrepreneurs were dubbed "The Mission Boys," who had arrived in Hawaii in 1825 with the missionaries.

There is an old, but apropos saying in Hawaii: "The missionaries came to do good, and they did very, very well."

When the Civil War ignited, the North lost its access to cotton from the Southern states and the Caribbean. The Union Army was desperate for cotton for uniforms and badges, and this created an opportunity for the new landowners of Hawaii.

Hawaii was now the closest and friendliest source of both sugar and cotton. Fortunes were made in the war years by the new landholders in Hawaii.

Growers of sugar and cotton eventually had to decide what their major crop was going to be. Sugarcane was far easier to grow in the island climate. Cotton was more susceptible to the many tropical pests, particularly the voracious pink bollworm.

With the choice made, cotton soon went into a downward spiral, and eventually dwindled to a mere 80 acres being planted in 1910.

Chapter 21

Hawaii Fun and Games

Hawaiians were a naturally fun loving people. They loved their festivals and games. There were markets and fairs held for the purposes of trade, and occasional public meetings for the discussion of national affairs, but the big annual festival was the *Makahiki*, or harvest festival, held in the autumn of the year.

In ancient Hawaii, roughly one third of the year was set aside as the "*makahiki*". During this four-month season, which began in the month of *Ikuwa* (roughly late October to early November), warfare was forbidden.

It was a time of playing games, celebrating the harvest, paying tribute to the chiefs, and honoring the god *Lono.* It was a time for storytelling, competitions, feasting, and dancing.

The old Hawaiians loved their leisure time. They harbored a treasury of games. Many of these demanded acute sharpness of verbal and mental skills. Gambling added spice and excitement to them.

Alii (chiefs) have been known to gamble away their land, while common men have bet their own lives, or the life of a mate. Missionaries frowned deeply on this behavior and discouraged the games. Gradually the Hawaiian games disappeared from the islands.

A contestant mounts his *holua (sled)* to compete in one of the ancient Hawaiian games.

One of the most popular old games is *konane*, a sort of checkers, played on a board, or on a slab of lava and rock. The *Makahiki* was devoted to games and gambling. There was boxing, foot racing, bowling, wrestling, surf swimming, a sort of tobogganing, and throwing and catching of the spear.

Another favorite was cock fighting, and there was a game that involved shooting of mice with a bow and arrow. This last event was confined to the chiefs as contestants.

A favorite amusement of the chiefs was sliding down hill on a long narrow sled: this was called *holua*; similar to a ski used in snow. The sled was made to slide on one runner, and the chiefs prostrated themselves on it.

For this sport they had a smooth trench dug from the top of a steep hill and down its sides, to a great distance over the adjoining plain. Dry grass was laid over the bottom of the trench, allowing contestants to reach high velocities going down the hill.

There were also games of an impure nature, played under the cover of darkness that included the dancing of the *hula-hula* but sometimes in a more lascivious manner than is currently enjoyed.

Moko-moko (boxing) was the favorite national game of the Hawaiians. It was regulated by fixed rules and presided over by referees or umpires. The champions generally belonged to different chiefs or districts, and crowds of partisans attended the events.

Sometimes, up to ten thousand spectators attended the matches. Deafening yells, dancing, and beating of drums followed a knockdown or blow that caused blood to flow. The elated victor strutted around the ring, challenging all comers to a contest, until he met his match. It was not infrequent that contestants would be left dead during one of these games.

A less fatal contest at the festivals was that of *hakoko*, or wrestling. A favorite sport also was *maika,* a form of bowling. In this game, a *kahua* or level track about three feet wide and a half-mile in length was made smooth and hard. Two short sticks were fixed in the ground only a few inches apart.

A player was required to bowl a circular, highly-polished stone, three or four inches in diameter, down the track and between the two sticks. Another version was to see which contestant could slide the stone the furthest down the track. The best players could bowl the stone upwards of a hundred rods.

Both men and women loved betting on their favorite contestants and did not hesitate to stake every article they possessed on the outcome of their favorite. It was indeed the betting opportunities as much as the sporting events that attracted the islanders.

Females would wager their beads, scissors, cloth-beating mallets, and every piece of cloth they possessed, except what they wore. The men were likewise daring, staking the tools of their trade, such as canoe making or farming implements, on the outcome of a match.

The games seldom ended without fierce brawls between the different parties.

This chant about the surf rider *Mamala* was translated from Hawaiian.

"The surf rises at Koolau
Blowing the waves into mist,
Into little drops,
Spray falling along the hidden harbor.
There is my dear husband Ouha,
There is the shaking sea, the running sea of Kou,
The crab-like moving sea of Kou.
Prepare the awa to drink, the crab to eat.
The small konane board is at Hono-kau-pu.
My friend on the highest point of the surf.
This is a good surf for us.
My love has gone away.
Smooth is the floor of Kou,
Fine is the breeze from the mountains.
I wait for you to return,
The games are prepared,
Pa-poko, pa-loa, pa-lele,
Leap away to Tahiti
By the path to Nuumealani (home of the gods)
Will my lover (Ouha) return?
I belong to Hono-kau-pu,
From the top of the tossing surf waves.
The eyes of the day and night are forgotten.
Kou has a large konane board.
This is the day, and to-night
The eyes meet at Kou."

This is the story:

Kou was a noted place for sports and games of chiefs long ago. East of Kou was a pond with a beautiful grove of coconut trees belonging to the chief, Hono-kau-pu. In this area were the finest surf waves of old Honolulu. This surf bore the name of *Ke-kai-o-Mamala* (The sea of Mamala). When the waves were high, it was known as *Ka-nuku-o-Mamala* (The nose of Mamala).

Mamala was a chiefess of *kupua* character, meaning that she was a *mo-o*, or gigantic lizard, as well as a beautiful woman. She was able to assume whichever shape she desired. One of the legends says that she was a shark and a woman, and had for her husband a shark-god, *Ouha.*

Mamala and Ouha played konane on the large smooth stone at Kou, and drank awa together. Mamala was known as a very skillful wave rider, the people on the beach would respond with applause over her athletic feats.

The chief of Hono-kaupu chose Mamala as his wife, so she left Ouha to live with her husband. Angry, Ouha tried to injure both of them, but was driven away. He fled to *Ka-ihi-Kapu* where he appeared as a man offering shrimp and fish to the women of the area.

The shrimp and fish escaped his basket, and the women ridiculed the god-man. Ouha could not endure the shame of this, and cast off his human form becoming the great shark god of Waikiki.

It should be noted that if a chant was said wrong or sung off key, this was a capital offense.

106

Chapter 22

Ancient Beliefs in Everyday Life

The ancient islanders were a superstitious lot and idol worship entered into virtually everything they did, even in everyday life.

A fisherman, for example, could never use a new net or fishing rod without praying and sacrifice to his patron god. He especially had to worship and offer sacrifices to the shark god.

When an islander built a house, it called for the advice of a *kilokilo*, or diviner, to be consulted as to the position and direction of the house. The *kilokilo* even advised on the arrangement of the sticks composing the framework. Hawaiians believed that sickness or death would ensue if they did not get this advice.

If it were a chief's house, human sacrifices might be required. This caused many people to flee to the mountains at such times to guard against their being chosen for such an offering. Most human sacrifices in the ancient Hawaiian customs were either prisoners taken in war or persons accused of a violation of some of the numerous regulations or *taboos*. Women seem to have been exempt from sacrifice.

Even the building of a canoe was very serious business. The whole operation had to be superintended by a *kahuna kalaiwaa*. The kahuna paid great attention to the choice of tree, and to the actions of birds, particularly the little *elepaio*.

An ancient Hawaiian *heiau or* temple at Waimea, Kauai

Before the tree was cut down, offerings of pork, red fish, coconuts, *awa*, and prayers were addressed to the gods. Another ritual with the gods took place before the finished canoe was dragged to the shore.

When the canoe was ready for launching, a final sacrifice, called the *lolo*, was offered while the owner was standing at the bow of the canoe.

If the silence during the ceremony was broken by any noise or anyone coming, it was considered a fatal omen, foreboding death and disaster, but if the silence was not broken, the canoe was considered safe.

Those engaged in agriculture were careful to plant on certain days of the moon. The *o-o*, "digger stick", had to be fashioned with prayers addressed to *Ku-pulupulu* or *Ku-moku-halii*, to insure good luck.

Prayers had to be repeated at planting, at various stages during the growth of the crop, and most certainly at harvest, when the first fruits were offered to family gods on the proper day of the moon.

Funerals were another matter. At the death of the king, the whole district was considered polluted for ten days, so that the heir to the throne was obliged to go to another district during this tabu period.

The *kuni* sorcerers first had to avenge the chief's death. A human sacrifice, called the *moepuu* was then offered to allow the king to enter the other world with attendance suitable to his rank.

One custom, besides the long and continued wailing, was for mourners to knock out one or more of their front teeth and cut their hair in grotesque shapes. Some tattooed their tongues, and others burned semicircles on their bodies in different places with burning bark.

While there were prayers connected with virtually every aspect of the Hawaiian's life, there were no religious ceremonies connected with marriage.

Chapter 23

Hawaii's Medicine Men

Ordinary cases of illness, in Hawaiian lore, were caused at the displeasure of the *aumakuas*. These were tutelary deities, or guardians, attached to particular families, and were generally, but not always, deified ancestors.

The ancient Hawaiian health system was well developed. They had a medical profession, medicines and treatments, and a lengthy apprenticeship program for medical specialists (*kahuna*)

To ancient Hawaiians, *mana* (spiritual power) was necessary to be a truly successful practitioner. If a parent sensed a child had a "healing spirit" enabling him to become a doctor, the child would be sent to live and study with a *kahuna* when as young as five years of age and they would spend as much as fifteen to twenty years in training.

During this time, they studied anatomy, learned how to diagnose disease, how to choose the right cures or medicines, and learned sacred prayers. They also learned how to perform simple surgical procedures, set bones and perform autopsies. They employed steam baths, massage, and laxatives to the patient and undertook empirical research.

Hawaiians believed the body could not be healed without healing the spirit. Before a patient was treated, the *kahuna* performed a ritual of *hooponopono* (making things right). This was a type of counseling with the aid of prayer to cleanse the mind and heart of negative thoughts and feelings.

The *aumakuas* watched zealously for any infringement of the tabus, and especially for any neglect to fulfill a vow.

If a chief was ill, offerings and prayers were made in the heiau, and chapels were built for the healing gods *Lonopuha* and *Koleamoku*. If the chief's illness was severe, human sacrifices were offered to the tutelary god of his family.

Vegetable remedies were used, but they were to provide a vehicle or medium through which the spirit would act, rather than having any curing power of their own.

There were many omens by which the *kahuna* (a professional, physician or priest) judged whether the patient would recover or not. After prayer and sacrifices, the *kahuna* would go to sleep to receive dreams or visions from his *akua* (spirit or god) on what remedy to use, or perhaps to ascertain what caused the disease.

If it did not rain during the night, on the following morning a fire was kindled and a fowl was baked for the *aumakuas*, a dog for the men's eating-house and another for the women, each covered with five kapas.

These offerings were eaten afterward by the relatives of the patient, and prayers were offered to the *aumakuas* and the gods of medicine.

Sometimes the patient was treated to a steam bath by being seated upon a pile of heated stones strewn over wet leaves, while enveloped in kapas. The patient was then dipped into the sea.

If he did not improve, some squid, *hee*, was spread out all-night and baked in the morning. The *kahuna* then repeated the *pule hee* prayer, while some of the squid was fed to the sick man. If this did not relieve him, it was evident that something uncommon was at work, some malevolent *akua* sent by a sorcerer to destroy him.

Common Curative Plants

Aalii (Hopseed Bush): The leaves are used to treat rash, itches and other skin diseases.

Awa (Kava): Used for headaches, muscle pain and to induce sleep. Also used to treat chills, colds, and other lung problems.

Kalo (Taro): It is the single most important plant in Hawaiian culture. The cut raw rootstock is rubbed on wounds to stop bleeding and the cut raw petiole is used to relieve the pain and prevent the swelling of insect bites and stings. The corn is used to treat indigestion and as a laxative.

Ko (Sugarcane): The sap is used to sweeten herbal preparations and the juice from the shoot is used to treat lacerations.

Olena (turmeric):   Belongs to the Ginger family. The bulb is used for sinus and ear problems.

Pia (Arrowroot):   The raw starch was used in water for diarrhea, and when mixed with red clay, for dysentery.

As one can see from the rituals and treatments afforded patients in ancient Hawaii, it just didn't pay to get sick.

Chapter 24

American *Missionaries* *Arrive*

The first school opened by the missionaries in Honolulu in May 1820. (Hawaiian Mission Children's Society)

There is a saying that the missionaries "came with a Bible, and the Hawaiians owned the land. When the missionaries left, the Hawaiians owned the Bible and the missionaries owned the land."

Certainly there was some truth to this bromide, as some missionaries did prosper while serving in the Hawaiian Islands, some rising to

115

the point of being mentors to the King and the chiefs on the various islands.

The American mission movement came about in an unusual way. A Hawaiian boy, named *Opukahaia*, was orphaned during the wars of Kamehameha. In 1809, an American sea captain offered him passage to the United States, along with another island boy, *Hopu*.

On ship was a Yale man who taught *Opukahaia* some English. What he learned was just enough to convince him that he was terribly ignorant in matters of the world. When he went ashore, the young Hawaiian looked for more instruction at Yale, from which his shipboard mentor was schooled.

He was fortunate. Samuel J. Mills, one of the leaders in the growing movement to send American Protestant missionaries overseas, heard about *Opukahaia* and decided he should be trained to return to his native Hawaii as a Christian teacher.

Opukahaia continued his English studies but also enrolled in the Foreign Mission School at Cornwall, Connecticut. He was a model student. He translated the Book of Genesis into Hawaiian, and began to work on a Hawaiian grammar, dictionary and spelling book.

Before he could begin his missionary teachings, *Opukahaia* fell ill with typhus. Before dying, he admonished his fellow students to love God and continue with the important work. His death actually strengthened the desire of supporters of the American Board of

Commissioners for Foreign Missions to evangelize the Hawaiian Islands.

Most missionaries were educated, and often college graduates. There were doctors, farmers, teachers and other recognized vocations. Many sacrificed lives of relative ease to travel to Hawaii, spending as much as a year on a leaky ship and tolerating the rough seas. For this, they traded their comfortable homes for grass huts in the most primitive land one could imagine.

It took 159 days of sailing before the Thaddeus arrived in sight of the snow-capped Mauna Kea on the island of Hawaii. The missionaries were quite unprepared for the appearance of destitution, degradation, and barbarism, among the clustering, almost naked savages.

The pioneer missionaries arrived at Kailua, Hawaii on March 30, 1820. Included were Hiram Bingham, of Vermont, and Asa Thurston, of Massachussetts. On their arrival, these missionaries were unaware that King Kamehameha had only recently died and was replaced by his son, Liholiho.

They learned, too, that Liholiho had abolished the rigid taboos that had been in place, forbidding men and women to eat together and not allowing women to eat pork or bananas, among other foods.

In the minds of New Englanders, Hawaiians were savages as well as sinners; the missionaries would have to "civilize" and "save" them all at the same time. In minister Bingham's opinion, the 40 years of association between the Hawaiians and the white whalers had only deepened the natives' depravity.

When informed of their purpose, Liholiho granted the missionaries permission to remain in Hawaii for one year. He feared agreeing to a longer time lest they would assume control of the islands. In giving permission, however, Liholiho ruled that the group must be separated.

Half of them would remain at Kailua, where Liholiho could keep his eyes on them, and the rest could go to Honolulu, the preferred place to live. Bingham and Thurston were both ordained ministers. Bingham therefore took one group to Honolulu and Thurston remained with another group at Kailua.

Natives came to the mission schools, more out of curiosity than an urge for schooling. A few stayed, but most found the constraint of clothing and the pain of literacy unbearable. The missionaries found it hard to understand Hawaiians, and harder still to love them. They abhorred the fact that Hawaiian women simply found work a "disgrace", yet these same women would practice the lascivious hula for countless hours.

As if lewd dancing and public nakedness were not bad enough, the missionaries witnessed polygamy being practiced everywhere. Even more upsetting was the incest being practiced by some Hawaiian royalty to insure there would be a proper royal heir.

Even with the relaxing of the *kapus,* many islanders kept their old ways. They prayed "people to death," warning the villagers that if they ignored the *kapus* everything would dry up for want of rain. The Christians were pleased every time heavy showers fell, but they needed allies more directly responsive than the weather.

They had planned to enlist the aid of the chiefs. But at the same time, they had no interest in propping up a savage despotism based on inherited rank. As good Christians, they did not believe the soul of a chief was worth more to God than the soul of a commoner.

King Liholiho was so erratic in his behavior that the missionaries could not count on him for help. On the one hand, he would announce that as the head of the islands, he had to be the most accomplished scholar. He might then assign intelligent young men like John Ii and David Malo to take his classes for him. Telling them to do his learning for him would be the same thing, he said.

He refused to accept the concept that the earth was round, instead of flat as he and his islanders believed. He would joke by warning his people to watch out for their calabashes tipping over as the earth turned over.

The most formidable task undertaken by the wives of the missionaries was the recording of the Hawaiian language so that the scripture could be translated and Hawaiians taught to read both Hawaiian and English.

Whalers, sailors and other entrepreneurs were not always happy with the restrictions the missionaries sought to enforce. Once, when missionaries on Hawaii were sailing away for a meeting in Honolulu, they looked back to see flames soaring toward the sky.

They had little doubt that it was one of their dwelling huts that was burning. Later, it was found that it was actually their small church that had been set afire by an arsonist.

There were reports that the mourning of the people over the burning of the church was the greatest since the death of Kamehameha. The fire thus only hastened the work of starting a new stone church. The church was completed in 1837, built of black stone and mortared with white coral.

Most of the native chiefs took a great interest in the work of the missionaries, particularly in the educational work. It was more difficult, however to arouse their interest in the new religion.

One of the first real converts was *Keopuolani*, the queen mother. Another was *Kapiolani*, a high chiefess who gave testimony to her Christian faith by publicly defying the dreaded goddess *Pele* at the volcano Kilauea.

The first to be baptized was the queen mother *Keopuolani*. The ritual was performed one hour before her death.

Childbirth in Ancient Hawaii

The Kahuna Ho-Ohanau was the equivalent of our obstetrician. He examined the mother-to-be at intervals. If the baby was in the wrong position, he oiled his hands with kukui oil and manipulated it. The mother's diet was regulated from the fourth month. She should eat greens and herbs to build up her baby's body. Salty foods were not allowed, only a little raw fish. After the sixth month, the mother was to eat lightly lest she have trouble at birth with a large baby.

Confinement

On the day of confinement many relatives gathered. The expectant mother was encouraged to walk to and fro until pain became intense. She then took a kneeling position with both knees apart. No Hawaiian woman dared scream in pain, lest she become the talk of the neighborhood. The Kahuna took charge. He sent someone to the beach to get morning glory leaves. The mother ate some; others were rubbed on her abdomen. After delivery the placenta was washed and buried under a tree. The mother was given warm broth and herbs, and her abdomen wrapped with tapa.

Birthplaces of Alii *(Holoholoku Wailua, Kauai)*

The birth of a high chief's child entailed elaborate ceremonies. Each island had its sacred birthstones. The most famous were: Holoholoku, Kauai and Kukaniloko on Oahu. Chiefs born there enjoyed special distinction. The chiefess gave birth leaning against reclining stones. Surrounding her were 36 stones on which sat royal midwives. If the baby was a girl, her cord was cut in the house. If a boy, he was taken to a *heiau* where the kahuna cut the cord with a bamboo knife. Offerings of pig, coconut and tapa were made. The kahuna said a special prayer. The child was taken back to the house, a wet-nurse was chosen as its "kahu". The kahu took great care in feeding the child. A tabu drum was sounded to announce the royal birth.

Chapter 25

The Progress of Education

Schools became very popular. As the brighter pupils learned to read, they were sent to open schools in neighboring school districts. One missionary gave this account on how the schools were spread.

Moo, the son of chief *Hoapili*, was considered a scholar. His father sent him to Hawaii to be a teacher for the district of Puna. As soon as his scholars had made a little proficiency, he sent the best of them out to be teachers in other schools. He continued doing this until every village of Puna was furnished with a teacher. A similar process was going on from Hawaii to Kauai.

As early as 1826, there were four hundred native teachers. Ten years after the coming of the missionaries, one third of the entire population was enrolled in the schools. Most of them learned to read, part of them learned to write, and a few learned the first principles of arithmetic.

One of the strange things about the schools was the fact that all but a few students were adults. In 1829, for instance, on the island of Oahu, only about one-tenth of the pupils were children.

The adult students had such a desire to learn the *palapala*, a name given by the Hawaiians to the system of teaching, that teachers could give little attention to the children. Parents did not want their children to go to school until they themselves had learned to read.

Schools reached their greatest development about 1832. Most of the people who were interested had gotten all the knowledge that the native teachers could give them. The schools began to dwindle away. Many of the schoolhouses were abandoned and fell into decay.

16

He popoki huhu.   He ilio hae.

E na pokii; e akahai; e akahele; mai hailiili; mai kuamuamu; mai hakaka me ka inaina; mai nuku aku kekahi i kekahi; e waiho i na hua hilahila.

Mai huhu hala ole aku ia hai. Ua huhu hala ole o Kaina i kona kaikaina ia Abela, a pepehi iho la ia ia.

Mai hoomaewaewa iki aku. Ua hoomaewaewa kekahi poe kamalii i ke kaula maikai ia Elisai, a ua make lakou i na holoholona hihiu hae; kanahakumamalua ka i make.

I mai la Iesu, Ua hoopuni mai na ilio ia'u, ua o mai lakou i ko'u mau lima, a me ko'u mau wawae.

A page from the first book printed for children in the Hawaiian language

The missionaries were paying more attention to the children and making special efforts to bring them into schools. Classes for children were organized at various mission stations. A first book for children was published in December 1829, and a copy was given to each boy and girl who came to school.

Schools received a big move forward when Governor Hoapili of Maui proclaimed a law that all children over four years of age had to attend school.

Missionaries then turned their efforts to training better teachers. The U.S. sent a number of teachers to Hawaii to assume charge of this missionary work. Several high schools and boarding schools were also established.

The most important high school to be established was the seminary for boys at Lahainaluna, Maui. This school was expected to be the "grand nursery of education in the islands." It did not disappoint its originators.

A similar school for girls was later begun at Wailuku, Maui. One of its purposes was to bring up a class of young women who would be proper helpmates for the young men being educated at Lahainaluna, and who would set a good example in the making of Christian homes.

Chapter 26

Sugar Was Sweet for Spreckels

Claus Spreckels

Claus Spreckels emigrated from Germany to the United States, and became a grocer in New York City.

Spreckels was born into a poverty-ridden family in Germany, and as a child, was expected to do the work of an adult. He was 18 when he arrived in the U.S.

He later traveled west to San Francisco, where he set up another grocery, then became a brewer, and later opened a sugar refinery. He knew nothing about refining, so he returned to

Sugar mill at Spreckelsville on Maui

Germany and spent eight months working as a common laborer in a sugar refinery.

Spreckels was shrewd, and sometimes ruthless. He soon controlled most of the sugar refineries on the Pacific Coast.

Pending in Washington was a controversial piece of legislation known as the "Reciprocity Treaty." This treaty would raise the duty-free price of sugar by two cents a pound. Hawaii was exporting 13,000 tons of sugar to the U.S.

Spreckels was a major opponent of the Reciprocity Treaty between the U.S. and Hawaii, but when it passed, he hurried off to Honolulu to use the treaty to his benefit. Within three weeks time, he had purchased more than half of the 1877 sugar crop projected at 14,000 tons before the new price went into effect. This put Spreckels into the Hawaiian sugar business in a big way.

The sugar baron opened up the dry central plain of Maui, described then as a "dreary expanse of sand and shifting sandhills, with a dismal growth in some places of thornless thistles and indigo."

Claus bought a half interest in sixteen thousand acres of dry land on the Waikapu Commons, leased from the government another twenty-four thousand acres at Wailuku Commons, and then petitioned the government's cabinet for water rights.

The cabinet responded that it would give the water rights serious study. This wasn't fast enough for Spreckels. If the ministers could not make up their mind, Spreckels contended that King Kalakaua should ask them to step aside in favor of men of decision.

A week later, Spreckels was sharing a bottle or two of champagne with Kalakaua at his hotel. At two in the morning, Kalakaua had his cabinet ministers wakened so that they could submit their resignations.

Spreckels got his lease. In exchange he gave a gift of $10,000 cash and a $40,000 loan at seven percent interest to pay off some notes the king had running at 12 percent.

Spreckels was given thirty years to enjoy the benefit of water rights, to be followed by another thirty years if the government extended his lease.

The Spreckelsville Plantation at Maui was one of the sugar king's major achievements. There he converted barren, useless land to profitable sugar-producing land.

He became a significant employer on Maui. Most of his employees included the 55,000 Chinese workers who came to Maui during 1887 and 1890.

Spreckels increased the number of iron rollers in his mills, enabling more complete and efficient extraction of sugar, a change that is still in use today.

The Spreckels sugar mills had electricity even before Honolulu had electric lighting.

Chapter 27

Royalty and Rank

Achief's genealogy determined where he stood in the hierarchy. The rank of his mother and father counted equally. When it was impossible to find a woman of equal rank to marry, a high chief might marry his own sister.

The child born from such a union would increase the high rank of his parents.

Ancient Hawaiian culture demanded that sacred children like these had to marry other sacred children.

Chiefs were all powerful, holding life and death authority over the commoners. Most of them realized that they needed the commoners for support during wartime and to supply food and goods, so were careful in not putting too many to death.

The chiefs were easily identifiable from the commoners. They wore capes and cloaks made from thousands of brilliantly colored red and yellow feathers. Their helmets were also covered with the brilliant feathers.

If a commoner did not like the chief under whom he lived, he was free to leave and seek a home on the lands of another chief. It was unusual that a commoner would be pushed so hard that he rebelled against a chief.

There was one cruel and arrogant chief, however, in the district of Kau on the Island of Hawaii, who did bring a great deal of displeasure to his commoners. This chief would have his men row him out to the boats of the fishermen. He would commandeer the fishing catch of the commoners, who depended on these fish to feed and clothe their families.

Finally, the commoners had suffered enough. The next time the chief pulled alongside the fishermen's' canoe, the fishermen were ready. They hurled rocks they had secreted in the bottom of their own canoe into the chief's canoe with such force that the bottom was smashed. They then quickly paddled away, leaving the chief and his men to drown.

It was essential for a chief to know if the gods looked with favor on a planned ocean voyage, or whether or not he should wage war on a neighbor. If the issue was vital, it might call for human sacrifices to assure the god of the importance of the occasion.

Rituals were conducted at *heiaus*, or temples, erected from a massive pile of fitted boulders, standing ten or more feet high. On top of these boulder platforms were several houses. One house was for roasting of sacrifices, another might serve as a drum house, and another would be the dwelling house of the god being worshiped.

For commoners, there was no "marriage." There was no ceremony that solemnized the union. A union was simply a matter of mutual agreement and convenience.

Often, the first-born girl of a commoner family would be given to the mother's parents. If the child was a boy, he might be given to the father's parents. It was felt grandparents would have more time to devote toward education and learning aspects than would the parents.

Separate houses were built for women to use during their menstrual cycles. This was a time when the women were considered "unclean" and must stay isolated from the men.

King Kalakaua, the brother of *Liliuokalani*, wrote this about the native Hawaiians and their culture.

They knew but little of the arts as we know them now, and the useful and precious metals were all unknown to them; yet they made highways over the precipices, reared massive walls of stone around their temples, carried effective weapons into battle, and constructed capacious single and double canoes and barges, which they navigated by the light of the stars. They had no language either of letters or symbolism, but so accurately were their legends preserved and transmitted that the great chiefs were able to trace their ancestry back, generation by generation, to something like a kinship with the children of Jacob, and even beyond in the same manner to Noah, and thence to Adam. What wonder, then, that under their old kings the islands of Hawaii should have been the home of romance, and that the south wind should have sighed in numbers through the caves of Kona?"

("The Legends and Myths of Hawaii", page 320)

Chapter 28

The Annexation of Hawaii

Hawaii President Sanford Dole and
U.S. Minister Harold M. Sewall at
the annexation ceremony on August
12, 1898

The following report was filed by the ranking naval
officer present when the American flag was first
raised in Hawaii after its annexation.

U. S. FLAGSHIP PHILADELPHIA, Honolulu, Hawaiian Islands, August 14, 1898.

SIR: I have the honor to submit the following report on the participation of the forces under my command in the ceremonies attending the change of sovereignty of the Hawaiian Islands, which took place at noon on Friday, the 12th instant:

As the report of this important event will be a matter of record in the files of the Navy Department, and as occasion may occur hereafter to refer to it to know what was done by the naval force on that occasion, it is made more in detail than it would otherwise be.

The force under arms from the Philadelphia and Mohican attending the ceremonies consisted of four companies of infantry and two sections of artillery.

The Hawaiian National Guard met our force at the landing and escorted them to the front of the executive building, where they took position in column on the driveway leading to the front of the building, the head of the column being close to the official stand. The Hawaiian troops were in position, a battalion on each side of the head of column of our men. The official stand was in front of the executive building, one side for the Hawaiian officials, the other for the United States minister and his attaches and the officers of the Navy and Army. Colonel Barber, of the First New York Volunteers, was third in the line of precedence, as the

136

ranking officer of the army present and next to me. The remaining officers of the Navy and Army were seated according to rank, there being in all twenty officers of the Navy present on the official stand and five of the Army.

All the officials having been seated except the president and his cabinet, the United States minister and his attaches, myself, Colonel Barber, and four of the ranking naval officers, the ceremonies commenced by the entrance on the platform from the executive building of the president and his cabinet, followed a moment later by the United States minister and the American officials mentioned above. After all were seated, prayer was offered by the Rev. G. L. Pearson, of Honolulu. Minister Sewall then rose, and addressing President Dole, formally communicated to him the text and purpose of the joint resolution of Congress annexing the Hawaiian Islands to the United States. President Dole then formally tendered the sovereignty of the islands, with all the public property of the Hawaiian Government, to the United States through our representative, Minister Sewall, who accepted it in the name of the United States Government. The actual ceremony of exchanging flags was then begun by the Hawaiian band playing Hawaii Ponoi, the national anthem. Colors were sounded, and, a 21-gun salute was fired by the shore battery and by the Philadelphia and Mohican, after which the Hawaiian flag was slowly hauled down, all the spectators standing uncovered.

Minister Sewall then turned to me and requested me to perform the duty intrusted to me, of hoisting the United States flag, and upon signal from me, as had been prearranged, colors were sounded, the flagship band played the Star Spangled Banner, and the United States flag was slowly hoisted on the flagstaff of the central tower of the executive building, two smaller flags being hoisted at the corners of the building to provide for the possibility of the main halyards carrying away; and 21 guns were fired by the Philadelphia and Mohican and the shore battery when the flag had reached the truck, all the spectators standing uncovered. The Hawaiian flag was hauled down, and the large United States flag hoisted by four men from the Philadelphia and Mohican, two from each ship, directly from the inner corners of the platform.

After the 'United States flag bad been hoisted and the salutes had been fired Mr. Sewall made a short address, and then communicated the directions of the President continuing the present government officials in office until Congress should provide a form of Government for the islands.

The chief executive of the Hawaiian government was then sworn in by the chief justice, followed by the members of his cabinet, after which our men and the local troops marched to the drill grounds, where the military officers, including the staff officers of the chief executive, were sworn in.

The battalion from the Philadelphia and Mohican then returned to the ships, escorted to the landing by the local troops. This concluded the participation of the force under my command in the change of sovereignty of these islands.

I am much indebted to Lieut. A. G. Winterhalter, flag lieutenant, and to Lieut. Philip Andrews, flag secretary, for their assistance arranging the details of the ceremonies connected with the raising of our flag, and for seeing that they were properly carried out.

I am gratified to be able to report to the Department that the ceremonies throughout were a complete success in every particular, and were rendered very impressive and dignified by the simplicity and lack of ostentation of the carefully prepared programme. The battalion from the two ships presented a fine appearance, and it gives me great pleasure to congratulate the Department on the opportunity given the Navy to take such a prominent part in an important event in the history of our country.

Very respectfully,

J. N. MILLER,
Rear-Admiral, U. S. N.,
Commander in Chief Pacific Station.

The SECRFTARY OF THE NAVY,
Navy Department, Washington, D. C.

Chapter 29

The Big Five

Sugar cane brought economic stability to Hawaii, but along with it cam backbreaking labor. (Google Images)

N o group in Hawaii was more prominent than "The Big Five." The Big Five was made up of Alexander and Baldwin, American Factors, C. Brewer and

Company, Castle and Cooke, and Theo. H. Davies Company.

The Big Five acted as buying and selling agents for thirty-six of the Territory's thirty-eight sugar plantations. They not only supervised the cultivation and marketing of Hawaii's million tons of sugar, but they banked the funds for the plantations, advanced operating capital, and provided the necessary forms of insurance.

For these and other services, the Big Five received about two and one-half percent of the gross proceeds derived from the sale of sugar grown on the plantations. In addition to the sugar industry, some agents also represented the Hawaiian pineapple industry, which supplies about eight percent of the canned supply of pineapple.

In his book, "Hawaii, Restless Rampart," Joseph Barber, Jr. depicts the widespread interest of the Big Five. Big Five's principal income from the sugar and pineapple industries is not from agent's fees but from dividends declared by the plantations. Average annual income during the five-year period 1935-1939 was $115,000,000, or about ninety percent of the value of all Hawaiian products.

Essentially, the Big Five controlled Hawaii's economy. Their interlocking directorates and close cooperation allowed them to act as one great combine that dominated Territorial government and every aspect of the Island's political, economic and cultural life.

When the Big Five took over the bulk of the arable land in the islands in the early 1800s, they set up a plantation system. They forced most workers to live in company housing and work the plantations for miserable wages, under brutal working conditions.

The Big Five were criticized for forever taking money out of one pocket and putting it into the other. Not only were the Big Five stockholders of the plantations, but the plantations were also stockholders of the Big Five.

Sugar and pineapple composed only one phase of the business. The Big Five were also agents for freight lines, and thus acted as middlemen in the shipment of sugar, pineapple and other Hawaiian products, and for the importation of supplies needed in Hawaii.

Commissions on this business was said to average well over $200,000,000 annually.

The Big Five owned outright a chain of wholesale and retail stores, and the largest department store in Hawaii. In addition, they were agents for hundreds of mainland corporations, which released their products through the Big Five. This included everything from sardines to locomotives.

Barber explained that despite the complicated nature of Big Five activity, the corporate structure of these companies is essentially simple.

Stock capitalization amounts to less than $50,000,000 for all, or an average of under $10,000,000 each.

The Big Five took advantage of the rich years of the past to retire their bonds. Two of the Big Five companies were almost entirely family-owned, and the other three had relatively few outside stockowners.

Employers dealt severely with labor protesters and smashed every attempt workers made to improve their conditions. In 1920, when Japanese and Filipino plantation workers struck separately on the island of Oahu, the employers evicted them from their company-owned homes.

More than 12,000 workers and their families were forced to camp in Honolulu parks, where more than 150 died during an outbreak of influenza.

In 1924 and again in 1935, Filipino workers organized and struck again along racial lines. They faced the same fate as before. They were evicted from their homes and forced to live on Wailokou Beach. Their leaders were jailed.

The strike failed because the Japanese continued to work. This and other incidents demonstrated that racial unity was necessary for unions to make any progress in the islands. They realized they needed to be tied to the mainland West Coast waterfront on the one end, and integrated into the whole economy of Hawaii on the other.

In 1946, striking sugar workers employed the earlier lessons learned and achieved one of the biggest victories in International Longshore and Warehouse Union history.

Through 1948 and early 1949, the employers pushed wage cuts, and forced a 68-day lockout at one plantation. By this time, the Big Five felt ready for a showdown. They provoked a strike by holding out against the Hawaii longshoremen's demand for wage parity with their mainland counterparts.

The 157-day strike tested every segment of the union's organization in Hawaii, including the employer's refusal to go to arbitration, government scab-herding, and innumerable arrests of union workers.

The IWLU's eventual victory gave the Hawaii longshoremen the same kind of recognition and status won by the longshoremen in 1934. It brought their wages up to mainland standards and put the colonial wage theory to rest.

In sugar, postwar mechanization of field operations cut the labor force as wages spiraled thanks to collective bargaining with the militant ILWU. The first real break in the Big Five's tight commercial power came in the 1950s.

By the mid-50's strong undercurrents of change were evident. Mainland retailers–Long's, Woolworth, and Hartfield–were coming in and in certain cases, introducing a type of price competition entirely new to Hawaii.

In 1974, however, none of the new lines of endeavor for the five was as profitable as was sugar. Soaring world prices and the lack of a national sugar act combined to ring up record profits.

Trust companies began to have some success in slowly unloading the holdings of Hawaiian securities in their trust accounts. This removed estate administrators, living by the "Prudent Man" rule, from the Big Five boardrooms, and the Big Five was losing its clout.

Chapter 30

Hawaii's Music and Dance

To Hawaiians, hula or Hawaiian dance, is as much a celebration of life as it is a proud statement of cultural identity. According to legend, hula originated when *Pele*, the Hawaiian goddess of fire, commanded her younger sister *Laka* to dance.

Schools were begun in honor of the goddess of the dance and temples were dedicated to her. Dancers lived on the temple grounds, subjected to strenuous training regimes and kapu (taboos) befitting the sacred art of hula.

Hula was the method in which ancient Hawaiians passed along the stories and legends of their culture to subsequent generations. Hula *kahiko*, or ancient hula, uses dance and chanting to relate the proud and somber history, customs, ceremonies and traditions of ancient Hawaii and her people.

Hula *auwana*, or modern hula, is the dance form most people are familiar with, combining dance and music for a more playful, joyous and spirited recounting of contemporary life in the islands.

Missionaries who arrived in the islands in the 1820s thought the hula too suggestive and outlawed it as a pagan practice. However, during the reign of King David Kalakaua (1874-1891), there was a resurgence of the old Hawaiian customs, including sports activities and hula.

"Hula is the language of the heart and therefore the heartbeat of the Hawaiian people," Kalakaua once said. Fashioning clothing from kapa or bark cloth was a duty belonging to the village women. It was a laborious task to make cloth out of the inner bark of certain trees and plants, such as breadfruit trees, the paper mulberry or *wauke* plants.

Today, people from different cultures and all walks of life eagerly spend hours researching chants and practicing dance techniques as part of a hula *halau* or house of hula instruction, perpetuating the respect, love and sharing that are as essential to this dance art as the movements, words and music.

Kapa Making

Men climbed to the wet highlands to harvest *mamaki*, sometimes as high as 4,000 feet, or they grew *wauke* in the lowlands.

After the outer bark was stripped away, the inner bark was soaked for several days in fresh or salt water. Strips of bark were then removed from the water, laid over a stone and pounded into thick strips with a round pounder. After a second soaking, these thick strips would be laid on a wooden log or anvil, which was always made of hard wood. Kawau was a favorite wood for anvils because of the booming sound it made when the kapa was struck.

The booming anvils often told far-away listeners stories of what was happening in the village. Far-away kapa makers would repeat the story on their anvils to those even further away and, in this way, kapa makers sent a story around the island in a few hours.

Kapa beaters, frequently made of *kauila* wood, had four sides or faces, each smooth, polished and carved with a different pattern. A shark's tooth set in a bone handle or a piece of sharp stone was used to do the carving.

When the kapa was finished, it was often dyed, painted or stamped with colored designs. Berries, bark, roots and even the soot from burning kukui nuts were used to create dyes in shades of gray, brown, blue, red and yellow. Paintbrushes were made from *hala* fruit, and stamps were made from bamboo. In this way, regular designs were repeated.

Since kapa was more like paper than cloth, the Hawaiians would soak it in kukui nut oil and coconut oil to give it additional protection from the rain. Kapa was often laid away with sweet smelling things, which would impart their natural perfumes to the cloth.

Lei Making

The magical history of the floral lei dates back to the ancient Hawaiians who wore braided leaves, native flowers, shells, feathers, stones and bones to beautify themselves.

They also offered these hand-made garlands to each other and to their gods as a symbol of love and friendship. The lei was treasured and worn with pride by people of every age.

During the Boat Days of the late 1800's, the popularity of the lei grew as visitors who arrived by ship were greeted with aloha and presented with floral leis. Legends grew around the luck of the lei. It was said if a departing visitor tossed their lei into the ocean and it floated back to the beach, it meant that the person would someday return to the islands. Hundreds of leis could be seen floating in the crystal waters off of Diamond Head as a ship steamed away.

Today, the ancient tradition continues. The tender and beautiful lei is still carefully made by hand, weaving fragrant and colorful flowers and leaves together to create a work of art. Leis are worn on all special occasions and given to family and friends as gifts of love. The lei are a symbol of Hawaii.

Stringing individual flowers into a single strand or multiple strands and tying the ends together create the flower lei, a garland worn like a necklace. Lei may be wide and flat or thick and round.

It may not even be made of flowers at all, as is the case with the maile, a fragrant vine with shiny green leaves that is draped U-shaped around a person's neck or placed upon an altar.

In ancient Hawaii, the presence of lei signified special occasions, such as when villagers gathered to tread a taro patch prior to its planting or when they came together to celebrate their collective efforts to build someone's home. In this context, the presentation of a lei symbolized sharing.

The lei also figured into more formal ceremonies. Jasmine flowers or *pikake* are traditionally used in courtship and marriage. The flower was name "pikake" or peacock because Princess Kaiulani had jasmine bushes and peacocks in her garden. The *pua kika* or cigar lei, made of hundreds of tubular red-orange flowers

151

strung in a spiral pattern, are presented to bridegrooms.

The *Ilima*, which is the flower of Oahu, ranges in color from yellow to deep gold to bright orange. This velvety lei requires 2,000 delicate and easily bruised flowers, which must be picked unopened before dawn and strung before they bloom in late morning. Often associated with, but not restricted to royalty, strands of Ilima many feet long were said to have been presented each morning to the Hawaiian monarchs.

Traditional *haku-lei* styles, which require more skill than the average lei, have become popular once again. This technique involves setting or mounting the flowers face up amid greenery on a backing of banana or other natural fiber. The ends of the fibers are tied together to have the haku lei encircle the recipient's neck or head.

Today, in addition to weddings and special ceremonies, flower lei are most often presented to honor birthdays and graduations. Islanders also don the lei on May 1, which is May Day or Lei Day in Hawaii, and during the Aloha Week festivities that take place throughout the islands during the fall.

Chapter 31

Cook May Not Have Been First

Most history books about Hawaii assert that Captain James Cook discovered the Hawaiian Islands, quite by accident, in January of 1778.

Hawaii's 19th century historians, however, credit the Spanish with the discovery and initial mapping of these islands. Hawaiian legends, too, support the idea of earlier European contacts, chronicling visitors, shipwrecks and castaways in ancient times.

Indeed, when the officers and crews of Captain Cook's *Resolution* and *Discovery* first encountered the Hawaiian People, they immediately began to wonder if they were the first Europeans to visit these shores.

The opening comment on this subject was logged on January 19, 1778 by Cook himself, aboard the *Resolution*, the day before coming to anchor off Waimea, Kauai.

While still off the east side of the island, he wrote of the natives that came out in canoes, *"There was little difference in the casts of their color, but some considerable variation in their features, some of their visages not being unlike Europeans."*

He continued by stating that the people he met on Kauai were not "*acquainted with our commodities, except iron; which however, it was plain, they had.... in some quantity, brought to them at some distant period.... They asked for it by the name of Hamaite.*" It is interesting to note that a Spanish word for iron is "*Hematitas*".

The following day, with the ships safely anchored, Captain Cook, with a number of his officers and men, went on an excursion inland. It was at this time that Cook was formally greeted and given the official title or name of *Lono.*

That afternoon, at a *heiau* (temple) on the western side of Waimea Canyon, he was presented with what he called "*a piece of hoop iron, about two inches long, fitted into a wooden handle, which our people guessed to be made of the point of a broad sword.*"

On the morning of the 23rd, "*one of the midshipmen purchased of the natives a piece of iron, lashed into a handle for a cutting instrument. It appeared to be a piece of the blade of a cutlass, and had by no means the appearance of a modern acquisition; looking to have been a good deal used and long in it's present state.*"

At that time, Captain Clerk, of the *Discovery,* wrote: "*One of the Alii, or principle people, came on & made me a present of two small hogs; one of his attendants had 2 large, long iron skewers. I was not master enough of the language to learn the proper history of them...I should have been glad to know, but it was pretty well clear from them having them at all...that Europeans have sometime or other been in the neighborhood*".

154

On the *Resolution*, Lt. King wrote "*One of the Indians held his two forefingers across each other and pointed to the land; which we construed into the Spaniards having set up a cross on shore. These circumstances, however fell far short of proof.*"

A few weeks later, safely anchored at Kealakekua the crews had much more time to interact with the Hawaiians. Again they found iron. The flattened out breech pin of a gun and an iron dagger, which had been beat out by the natives, were seen in the village before Captain Cook was killed. The travelers discovered that the Hawaiians played a board game, much like our checkers.

In August of 1798, a trader named Ebenezer Townsend wrote that "*It is very much in doubt whether Capt. Cook was the first discoverer of these islands, it appears pretty evident that he was not.... There is at Mowee the ring and part of the shank of an anchor of about seven hundred weight.... where there is no recollection of their ever having been a vessel, and for it's appearance it must have been there many years.... They have a tradition that a couple of white men came on shore and remained there about a hundred and fifty years ago.*"

His Hawaiian Majesty, David Kalakaua, published his *Legends and Myths of Hawaii* in 1888. In that volume he tells us that during the reign of Kamaluohua on Maui there was another shipwreck there, from which there were five survivors, two women and three males.

Very few artifacts remain today that are certain to have come from pre-Cook European ships. Two, that have surfaced, were interred with the bones of an ancient chief, inside of woven casket called "*Ka'ai*". A piece of metal attached to a wooden handle, that appears to be a dagger, was found along with a piece of flaxen sailcloth, which dates to the 1600s.

Cloth, in its symbolic form was another thing that caused Cook's crews to wonder about possible western predecessors at these islands. The standard of the annual *Makahiki*, or harvest festival, was a tall cross, hung with long strips of cloth, somewhat resembling a ships mast and sails.

Another hint of prior contact were certain articles of chiefly attire. Captain Cook wrote: "*Amongst the articles which they brought to barter.... we could not help taking notice of a particular sort of cloak and cap, which, even in countries where dress is more particularly attended to, might be reckoned elegant. The first were nearly the size and shape of the short cloaks worn by the women in England, and by the men in Spain.*" Nothing of the kind existed elsewhere in Polynesia.

Lt. King wrote; "*The exact resemblance between this habit, and the cloak and helmet formerly worn by the Spaniards, appears to me sufficient proof of its European origin. We are driven indeed...to a supposition of the shipwreck of some buccaneer, or Spanish ship, in the neighborhood of these islands.*"

156

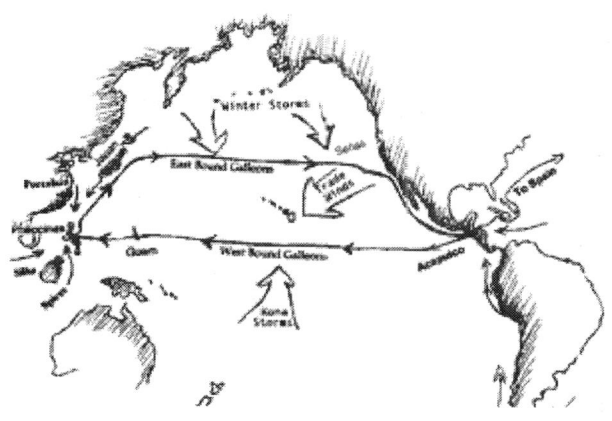

Map showing route of Spanish galleons.

Between 1565 and the 1800s, the Spanish maintained a colony in the Philippines. During most of those years, two ships would leave Acapulco, Mexico in the spring, sail down to about ten degrees north and then directly west towards Guam, which they would reach in about eight weeks.

After a short stay to restock with food and water they would continue on to Manila. These ships carried the colonists, soldiers and priests as well as the supplies necessary to keep the colony comfortable.

The primary cargo on this voyage was Mexican silver, which was used to pay the wages of the people and administrators of the colony as well as purchase the silk, porcelain, spices and other Asian goods needed in Mexico and Europe.

Large galleons, loaded with these Asian treasures would depart Manila in July, sail up to the latitude of Japan and cross the North Pacific. Seeing land near San Francisco, they would then sail down the coast, not stopping until they reached the colonies in Mexico, usually in January.

During the two centuries of galleon trade, nine vessels vanished without a trace. Could any of these have been wrecked in Hawaii?

No Spanish map has yet been found which shows the location of a shipwreck in the mid-Pacific. However, many maps show these islands. In fact most charts of the Pacific printed in Europe after 1570 show a group of Islands in this vicinity named "*La Mesa, Los Monges*, and *La Desgraciada*". "*The Table, The Monks*, and *The Unfortunate One*" are surely the Hawaiian Islands. Captain Cook had charts with him that showed these islands.

Lieutenant Henry Roberts was the draftsman aboard the *Resolution*. It was his duty to draw up all the charts and update any new cartographical information. He was commissioned to draw up a map of the world on the basis of the best information available on board the ships. That work was nearly complete at the time of Captain Cook's death.

There was some discussion amongst the ship's officers as to whether the Sandwich (Hawaiian) Islands and the *La Mesa* and *Los Monges* group were one in the same. Captain Cook, not having time to investigate further eastward, decided that both groups should be depicted. Further investigation was left to later explorers.

Some of Cook's officers returned to the Pacific before the turn of the 19th century and looked in vain for the *Los Monges* Islands. Captains

158

Portlock and Dixon came in 1786 on a fur-trading mission. George Vancouver followed in 1793.

The Frenchman, Laperouse was but a week behind Portlock and Dixon. He wrote, "*I thought it would render an important service to geography if I could succeed in erasing from the charts those idle names, denoting islands which have no existence, and perpetuating errors extremely injurious to navigation.*"

Once anchored in the Bay that bears his name to this day, Laperouse and a number of his officers and men went ashore. The Frenchmen soon noticed that some of the people showed signs of the venereal disease, syphilis.

The ship's surgeon, M. Rollin, examined a number of the people and found that they showed signs of having advanced cases of this disease, which, in Europe would have taken twelve to fifteen years to develop.

The fact that Cook had visited these islands but eight years prior and never landed on Maui at all, led Laperouse to conclude that the venereal disease was introduced in the islands before Cook's time.

Indeed, the men of Cook's ships wondered how the disease could have traveled so quickly, and spread so widely, amongst the Maui people, by the time of their arrival there, as they had left Kauai but nine months prior.

Modern archaeology supports the Frenchman's position. A few years ago, the remains of a young woman, known to have died before 1664, were unearthed on Oahu. Her bones showed signs of the congenital form of this disease.

Another notable find, made on Oahu, was a life-size carved stone image of a man in 17th century European dress, unearthed in Manoa Valley prior to the 1860s. Hawaiian Tradition is sometimes quite specific about certain events concerning foreigners.

Thomas Manby, who was with Vancouver, befriended an old Hawaiian priest while at Kealakekua. He later stated, "*This traditional historian informed me that a few generations back white men visited the Sandwich Islands, many of whom remained behind & were raised to the highest honors. From these visitors it is recorded that the present batch of Royalty are descended*."

In 1804, a fur trader named Captain Shaler wrote that several years before Cook's appearance "*a ship appeared off the south end of Owhyee; two girls went on board of her in a small canoe, which was stove alongside the ship, and after remaining a night on board, they returned in a small boat furnished them by the commander of the ship. This fact is so well averred (among the natives) that it cannot be doubted; and there is the greatest reason to suppose the ship was Spanish*."

In 1823, the Reverend William Ellis made a circuit of the Island of Hawaii and spent some time with the Governor of that island. From him and other informants, Ellis was able to gather enough information on this subject to write the following: "*They have three accounts of foreigners arriving at Hawaii before Captain Cook.... One tells of a priest who made changes in the Hawaiian religion, and of his son who spoke the*

160

same language as some other foreigners that came ashore later".

Another account states that in the reign of Kahoukapu, "*Seven foreigners arrived at Kearake'kua Bay, the spot where Captain Cook subsequently landed. They came in a painted boat, with an awning or canopy over the stern...The color of their clothes was white or yellow, one of them wore a pahi, long knife...at his side, and a feather in his hat. The natives received them kindly. They married native women, of Hawaii, which is said, was for some time governed by them.*"

It appears that this legend has a strong basis in fact and ties in with the only unquestionably documented European contact with the Hawaiian Islands before Captain Cook. In 1599 a fleet of five Dutch trading ships entered the Pacific bound for Japan. Two of these vessels, the *Lefda* and the *Hope*, reached the planned rendezvous off Chili.

They then directed their course for Japan. The *Lefda's* pilot, an Englishman named William Adams (upon whose life the novel *Shogun* was based), chronicled highlights of the ensuing voyage in two letters, which eventually reached London. He writes: "*We took our course directly for Iapan... in our way, we fell with certain islands in sixteen degrees of north latitude... comming neere these islands, ...eight of our men.... ran from us with the pinnesse.*"

The importance of cross-referencing legends with documents now allows us to state that Kahoukapu seems to have ruled in 1599.

In 1880 Abraham Fornander published his *Account of the Polynesian Race.* In that volume he wrote that " *In the time of Kealiikaloa, king of Hawaii and son of Umi, arrived a vessel at Hawaii. Konaliloha was the name of the vessel, and Kukanaloa was the name of the foreigner who commanded.... His sister was also with him on the vessel.*

As they were sailing along, approaching the land, the vessel struck at the Pali, and was broken to pieces by the surf, and the foreigner Kukanaloa and his sister swam to shore and were saved, but the greater part of the crew perished..."

The evidence for Spanish and Dutch contact with Ancient Hawaii, is overwhelming, however conclusive physical proof, in the form of a shipwreck eludes us. In time, we hope to prove conclusively that the English ships of 1778 were not the first Europeans to visit these shores.

Chapter 32

Hawaii's Unwanted Mongoose

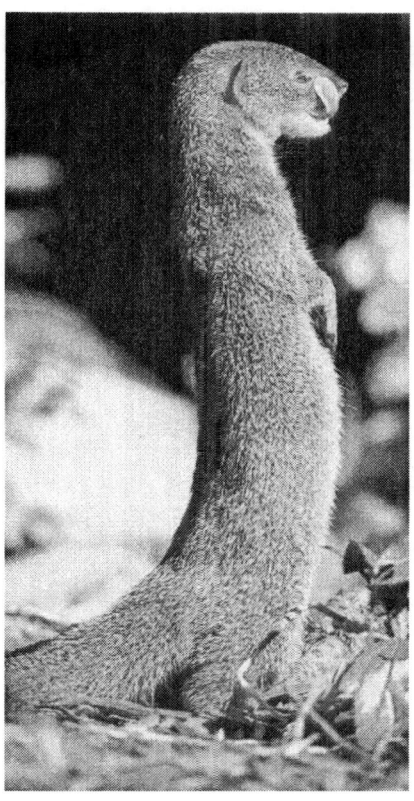

The Indian Mongoose is now
Hawaii's greatest pest.

The Indian mongoose was brought to Hawaii to kill rats in the sugar cane fields. The problem is the mongoose hunts during the day while the rats do their prowling at night.

Back in 1872 a man named W.B. Espeut got the idea that Indian mongoose might take care of the rat problem in Jamaica if turned loose in the sugar cane fields there. So he sailed across the ocean to Calcutta on a ship called the Merchantman, captured four male and five female mongooses (one pregnant) and brought them back across the ocean to Jamaica.

Twenty years later, in a journal article, Espeut gave the mongoose rave reviews. Besides killing rats, he wrote, "snakes, lizards, crabs, toads and the grubs of many beetles and caterpillars have been destroyed."

Espeut's paper captured the interest of Hawaii sugar planters, but not everyone was convinced that importing the mongoose was a good idea. Even as far back as 1883, in an issue of Planters Monthly, someone wrote, "Whether it would be wise to introduce the animal to these Islands may be a question. It would be important to first learn more of the nature of the creature, for they may prove an evil."

Unfortunately, no one heeded this anonymous writer's advice. That same year, 72 Jamaica mongooses were loaded onto a ship and sailed to the Hamakua Coast of the Big Island. Later, offspring of these animals were released on Maui, Molokai and Oahu.

One story says that Kauai officials didn't want mongooses on their island, and when a shipment reached there, the animals were thrown overboard in the harbor and drowned. To this day, Kauai hosts no mongooses.

But the other islands have them and it's been a disaster. Mongooses do eat rats, it turns out, but not enough to control rat populations. Sugar crops on Maui,

164

Oahu, Molokai and the Big Island suffered as much economic damage from rats as those on Kauai, which does not have the mongoose.

Far worse is the mongoose has a voracious appetite for ground-nesting birds and their eggs. Our much-loved nene, or Hawaiian goose, nearly became extinct due to mongoose predation. Mongooses also wiped out Newell's shearwaters on Oahu, Molokai, Maui and the Big Island.

Because Hawaii hosts no natural predators for mongooses, they have to be trapped or poisoned to keep their populations in check. Getting rid of them completely is nearly impossible. The mongoose is as strong a survivor as the rats they were brought here to eliminate.

All the mongooses in Hawaii today are descendants of those first nine animals brought to Jamaica. Females bear from one to three pups twice a year.

Mongooses (and rats) can carry a potentially lethal disease called leptospirosis. The bacteria are transmitted to humans through infected animals' urine that gets into ponds and streams—which of course, all eventually run into the ocean.

Chapter 33

The Endangered Species

Endangered Palila

Hawaii is considered the endangered species capitol of the world, with more endangered plant and animal species per square mile than any other place on the planet.

Hawaii is currently suffering a serious bird extinction crisis, which began during Polynesian settlement over 1,600 years ago, and continued through the period of European settlement in the late 1700's to today.

Hawaii's unique native birds and other animals are threatened by destruction of habitat for farming and human development, invasion of alien plant species, disease spread by introduced mosquitoes, predation by introduced rats, mongoose, and domestic cats, and habitat degradation by feral pigs, goats, sheep, and cattle.

Hawaii is the most isolated group of islands in the world. It is 2,400 miles to the nearest continent and the nearest group of atolls or low islands is 850 miles away.

Over the years, before the Europeans arrived in Hawaii, many species developed unique abilities and in turn many animals and plants evolved in Hawaii that couldn't be seen anywhere else in the world.

These species then became known as Hawaii's native or endemic animals or plants. The Hawaiian Islands isolated from the world started out barren and lifeless and was considered a paradise.

The first flora and fauna arrived by ocean waves and/or jet stream, by birds' droppings, and by hitchhiking on a piece of an object. The species adapted to the island environment. The animals and plants in Hawaii slowly evolved to be defenseless because they had no fear of predators.

Thorny plants such as the Hawaii raspberries, *'akala*, lost their thorns, the *ko'oko'okau* lost the barbs on its needles, some plants lost their strong scents, several birds lost their ability to fly, the birds' beaks changed their shape, and the root system of some plants became fragile.

Hawaii's flora and fauna lived a happy and peaceful life and many unique species evolved, but this all came to an end when foreign intruders arrived.

Cats were probably introduced to the Hawaiian Islands in the late 1700's, and now, feral and free-roaming cats are a significant problem, even in higher elevations far away from human development.

For example, the federally endangered Palila, a Hawaiian honeycreeper, is threatened by feral cats in their protected, but limited habitat of mamane and mamane-naio forest on Mauna Kea.

Biologists have been monitoring the Palila population for years and have found that since 1998, cats depredated 8 to 11 percent of monitored Palila nests annually. Cat predation inhibits efforts to restore the Palila population.

To learn more about the movements, ranges, and habits of feral cats in high elevation dry forests, biologists from the U.S. Geological Survey captured and attached radio collars to five male and three female feral cats and tracked them for 18 months.

Because of the cats' large home ranges, and immigration of new cats from lower elevations, they concluded that controlling feral cats in Palila habitat would be very difficult.

The 'Alala or Hawaiian Crow, is highly endangered. Endemic to the island of Hawaii, this crow was once abundant in the lower forests on the western and southern sides of the island. However, by the early 1990's, 'Alala could only be found in the Kona Forest Unit of Hakalau National Wildlife Refuge.

By October 1999, there were only three individuals left in the wild. A captive-breeding program was started in the 1970s, and by 1998,

24 birds had been released. However, 18 died and the rest were recaptured to protect them and preserve genetic diversity.

This bird has suffered from: over-hunting; loss and degradation of habitat; avian malaria and pox carried by introduced mosquitoes; predation by cats, rats, mongoose, and toxoplasmosis, a disease common to domestic cats and rats.

An environmental assessment has been prepared, and other potential release-sites are being investigated, but it is difficult to find a viable site for 'Alala anywhere on the island.

(The information in this chapter was adapted from the American Bird Society's web site)

Chapter 34

The 'Poi Clippers' of Hawaii

Matson's luxury liner Lurline traveled California to Hawaii route.

(Google Images)

Travel by sea has always been of first importance by the people of Hawaii. The king and chiefs of Hawaii owned vessels, and the government was involved in the shipping business until 1846.

Beginning about 1820, many small ships were owned by local people and operated among the islands. None of these ran on fixed schedules and the hazards of the sea and lack of navigation made traveling to another island a minor miracle.

Traveling in these "poi clippers," as they were called, meant long, rough and crowded conditions. Passengers in the cabins of these vessels were driven to seek fresh air on the narrow decks. These decks, too, were jammed with steerage passengers and a mixed cargo.

A typical load for these vessels might be similar to one reported by a Honolulu newspaper in 1853. *The schooner Pau, took 290 passengers to Hawaii, and brought back 190, along with 20 turkeys, 30 pigs, 75 chickens, 30 dogs, 1 pair oxen, 1 mule, 14 cords of wood, and 11 canoes among other things.*

Freighting carried on by the small vessels sailing among the islands became an expanding business. Cargoes of sugar, molasses, wheat, and firewood were transported to Honolulu and imported goods were shipped back.

In 1851, there were sixty-five coasting ships, averaging about sixty tons, registered under the Hawaiian flag. Sailing ships offered the steamers stiff competition on freight through the end of the 19th Century, even when steamers were functioning well.

Steamers won the bulk of the passenger traffic, mail and some freight. But sailing ships could carry freight at less cost. In 1860, two new sailing ships were added to the coasting fleet.

First to arrive was the clipper ship *Emma Rooke,* followed in a month by the schooner *Nettie Merrill.* Coasters often kept irregular and unpredictable schedules, going where paying freight took them. However, some served specific ports with a degree of regularity.

Matson Navigation Company's long association with Hawaii began in 1882, when Captain William Matson sailed his three-masted schooner Emma Claudina from San Francisco to Hilo, Hawaii, carrying 300 tons of food, plantation supplies and general merchandise.

That voyage launched a company that has been involved in such diversified interests as oil exploration, hotels and tourism, military service during two world wars and even briefly, the airline business. Matson's primary interest throughout, however, has been carrying freight between the Pacific Coast and Hawaii.

In 1887, Captain William Matson sold the Emma Claudina and acquired the brigantine Lurline, which more than doubled the former vessel's carrying capacity. As the Matson fleet expanded, new vessels introduced some dramatic maritime innovations.

The bark Rhoderick Dhu was the first ship to have a cold storage plant and electric lights. The first Matson steamship, the Enterprise, was the first offshore ship in the Pacific to burn oil instead of coal.

Increased commerce brought a corresponding interest in Hawaii as a tourist attraction. The second Lurline, with accommodations for 51 passengers, joined the fleet in 1908. The 146-passenger ship S.S. Wilhelmina followed in 1910, rivaling the finest passenger ships serving the Atlantic routes.

More steamships continued to join the fleet. When Captain Matson died in 1917 at 67, the Matson fleet comprised 14 of the largest, fastest and most modern ships in the Pacific passenger-freight service.

When World War I broke out, the government requisitioned most of the Matson fleet as troopships and military cargo carriers. Other Matson vessels continued to serve Hawaii's needs throughout the war.

After the war, Matson ships reverted to civilian duty and the steamers SS Manulani and SS Manukai were added to the fleet – the largest freighters in the Pacific at that time.

The decade from the mid-20s to mid-30s marked a significant period of Matson expansion. In 1925, the Company established Matson Terminals, Inc., a wholly owned subsidiary, to perform stevedoring and terminal services for its fleet.

With increasing passenger traffic to Hawaii, Matson added the S.S. Malolo in 1927. The Malolo was the fastest ship in the Pacific, cruising at 22 knots. Its success led to the construction of the liners Mariposa, Monterey and Lurline between 1930 and 1932.

Immediately after the December 7, 1941 attack on Pearl Harbor, the passenger liners Lurline, Matsonia, Mariposa and Monterey, and 33 Matson freighters were called to military service.

The four passenger liners completed a wartime total of 119 voyages, covered 1 1/2 million miles and carried a total of 736,000 troops. The post-war period for Matson was somewhat difficult.

The expense of restoration work proved to be very costly and necessitated the sale of the Mariposa and Monterey, still in wartime gray. In 1948, the Lurline returned to service after a $20 million reconversion.

Two new Matson hotels were built on Waikiki in the 1950s, the SurfRider in 1951 and the Princess Kaiulani in 1955. In 1955, Matson undertook a $60 million shipbuilding program which produced the South Pacific liners Mariposa and Monterey, and the rebuilt wartime Monterey was renamed Matsonia and entered the Pacific Coast-Hawaii service.

Chapter 35

Hawaii's Volcanoes

A volcano blows its top

The Hawaiian Islands are volcanic in origin. The Hawaiian hot spot has created 82 volcanoes that stretch for more than 1,500 miles to form the Hawaiian Islands.

Source of this heat could lie as deep as 2000 miles underground. This "hot spot" is formed by magma (molten lava) punching through the tectonic plate and erupting continuously for at least some 70 million years to create the islands. As the plate moves away (at 5-10 cm/yr) the volcanoes stop erupting.

The Hawaiian Islands are moving across the Pacific Ocean at about the same speed that your fingernails are growing. The life of a Hawaiian volcano before it sinks back under the sea floor is between 5 and 10 million years.

The Big Island of Hawaii is constructed of 5 shield volcanoes: Kilauea, Mauna Loa, Mauna Kea, Hualalai, and Kohala. Mauna Loa is the largest active volcano and most massive mountain on earth, occupying an area of 10,000 cubic miles.

Mauna Kea, at 13,796 feet, is the highest. Kilauea (4093 feet) is the youngest and one of the world's most active with its satellite vent Pu'u O'o the source of the current lava flows. The Kilauea caldera is about two miles wide and more than three miles long.

Most of the Kilauea caldera formed shortly before and during the eruption of 1790. Calderas are large collapsed craters that are formed by magma draining away along the rift zones within the volcano. A caldera is the actual caving in of the top of the mountain.

As you move from the islands of Hawaii to Kauai, the volcanoes become older and older. Oahu's volcanoes have not erupted for a million years. There are three volcanoes that are active in Hawaii: Kilauea that has been active since 1983, Mauna Loa which last erupted in 1984 and Loihi, the submerged volcano that lies about thirty miles off the southern coast of Hawaii, 3,000 feet under the sea surface and is expected to emerge in a thousand centuries.

Legends of *Pele*, the goddess of volcanoes, tells about her search for a home, moving down the chain of islands digging her fire pits until she arrived at Kilauea where she made her home in the lava filled craters.

There are two types of lava flow: *'a 'a* and *pahoehoe*. 'A 'a is rough and clinkery with sharp, jagged rocks. Pahoehoe flows are fluid with less gas content so the surface appears smooth and sometimes ropy.

Lava tubes are formed in pahoehoe lava flows when the surface flows harden while the lava in the interior is still molten. The lava then drains out of the flow from below, leaving a tunnel or tube. Some tubes can be as large as a subway tunnel.

Hawaiian eruptions are generally non-explosive because the magma's high temperatures (1,200C) as it reaches the surface make it very liquid. They erupt not only at their summits but also along rift zones, which are fractured zones of weakness within the volcano. Kilauea has two rift zones.

The information for this story comes from the Hawaii Volcanoes National Park Service.

Chapter 36

The Attack on Pearl Harbor

A captured Japanese photo
shows Battleship Row during
the Pearl Harbor attack.
Hickam Field burns in the
background.

(Armed Forces photo)

The attacking planes came in two waves.
The first wave hit at 7:53 a.m., the
second at 8:55 a.m. An hour later, it
was all over. By 1 p.m., the carriers that had
launched the planes from 274 miles off the coast
of Oahu were heading back to Japan.

Behind them they left chaos, 2,403 dead, 188 destroyed planes and a crippled Pacific Fleet that included eight damaged or destroyed battleships.

Japanese planes hit just before 8 a.m. on December 7. Within a short time, five of eight battleships at Pearl Harbor were sunk or sinking, with the rest damaged.

Several other ships and most Hawaii-based combat planes were knocked out and more than 2400 Americans were dead. Soon after, Japanese planes eliminated much of the American air force in the Philippines, and a Japanese Army was ashore in Malaya.

President Franklin Roosevelt learned of the attack while having lunch in his oval study. He soon received a call from Winston Churchill informing him that the Japanese had also attacked British colonies in Southeast Asia and that Britain would declare war the following day.

Roosevelt responded that he, too, would go before Congress to ask for a declaration of war against Japan. This statement elated Churchill, who wrote:

> *To have the United States at our side was to me the greatest joy. Now at this very moment I knew the United States was in the war, up to the neck and in to the death. So we had won after all! ...Hitler's fate was sealed. Mussolini's fate was sealed. As for the Japanese, they would be ground to powder.*

The United States was supposedly at peace with Japan and, at the solicitation of Japan, was still in conversation with its government and its emperor toward maintaining peace in the Pacific.

Indeed, one hour after Japanese air squadrons had commenced bombing in Oahu, the Japanese Ambassador to the United States and his colleague delivered to the Secretary of State a formal reply to a recent American message. While this reply stated that it seemed useless to continue the existing diplomatic negotiations, it contained no threat or hint of war or armed attack.

Ten minutes after the beginning of the attack a bomb crashed through the USS Arizona's two armored decks, igniting its magazine. The explosion ripped the ship's sides open like a tin can, starting a fire that engulfed the entire ship. Within minutes she sank to the bottom, taking 1,300 lives with her.

The Japanese planes bombed all the U.S. military air bases on the island. The U.S. Army's Hickam Field was the largest.

Japan's purpose for attacking Pearl Harbor was to neutralize American naval power in the Pacific. Japan was embroiled in a war with China. It had already seized Manchuria.

Japan's invasion of southern Indo-China in mid-1941 provoked the U.S., Great Britain, and the Dutch colonial government, into imposing an embargo of strategic materials to Japan. This 'threat' to the Japanese economy (and military supplies) was intended to force them to reconsider the move into IndoChina and perhaps even to negotiate.

Planning had begun for a Pearl Harbor attack in support of further military advances in January of 1941. They could not expect the United States to remain unmoved by their plans when activated; it was this expectation which had led Yamamoto to consider a way to pre-emptively neutralise US power in the Pacific. His idea of an attack on the naval base at Pearl Harbor was one tactic to achieve this strategic goal.

One of the main Japanese objectives was the three American aircraft carriers stationed in the Pacific, but these had sortied from Pearl Harbor a few days before the attack and escaped unharmed.

In terms of its strategic objectives, the attack on Pearl Harbor was, in the short to medium term, a spectacular success which eclipsed the wildest dreams of its planners and has few parallels in the military history of any era.

In the longer term, however, the Pearl Harbor attack was an unmitigated strategic disaster for Japan. Most significantly of all, the Pearl Harbor attack galvanised a divided nation into action as little else could have done. Overnight, it made the whole of America utterly determined to defeat Japan, and it probably made possible the unconditional surrender position taken by the allied powers.

Glossary of Hawaiian Words

aina -- The land, earth.

'akahi -- One. (Especially when counting in a series.)

ali'i -- Ancient Hawaiian royalty.

aloha -- A greeting, also used when parting. Both hello and goodbye. Love.

'alua -- Two. Twice.

'au'au -- To bathe or take a shower. eg. Gotta go 'au'au after fishing all day.

'eha -- Four. Four times.

'ekahi -- One. Once.

'ekolu -- Three. Three times.

'elima -- Five. Five times.

'elua -- Two. Twice.

ewa -- An area west of Honolulu

hala -- The pandanus tree, whose leaves are plaited into mats, baskets and hats.

halau -- A long house for canoes or hula instruction.

hale -- House. eg. It's appropriate that Honolulu's City Hall is called Honolulu Hale.

hapu'u -- An endemic tree fern, common in many forests of Hawai'i, and now frequently cultivated.

haole -- Originally, a foreigner, but the term is now used mainly to depict blondes or caucasians.

hihiwai -- An endemic grainy snail found in both fresh and brackish water.

ho'oponopono -- To correct.

hui -- A club, association or group.

hukilau -- A net; to fish with a net.

hula -- A lovely Hawaiian dance form.

huli -- To turn or flip over.

humuhumu-nukunuku-a-pua'a -- This is Hawaii's state fish, whose nose is shaped like a pig's.

imu -- An underground oven.

kahuna -- A priest, minister or expert in any field.

kahuna lapa'au -- A healer or doctor.

kai -- Sea, near the sea.

kalua -- To bake in an underground pit or oven. Often used to describe pig served at lu'aus.

kama'aina -- A native-born or longtime Island resident.

kane -- Man or men. eg. Go through the door marked kane, not wahine.

keiki -- Child or children.

kiawe -- Algaroba tree. Like mesquite, its wood is often used to barbecue.

kokua -- Assistance, help. eg. We need your kokua. Please don't litter.

koloa -- Hawaiian duck.

konohiki -- Headman of an ahupua'a (land division).

kukui -- Candlenut tree bearing nuts containing oily kernels formerly used for lighting by ancient Hawaiians.

kuleana -- Small piece of property.

kumu hula -- Teacher of Hawaiian dance.

la'au lapa'au -- Medicine. Curing medicine.

laua'e -- A fragrant fern whose pieces were often strung in pandanus leis.

laulau -- A combination of pork, beef, chicken and/or fish, wrapped in luau leaves and steamed.

lei -- A flower necklace.

liliko'i -- Passion fruit used for desserts and beverages.

lokahi -- Unity. To blend opposites.

lomilomi -- Massage. eg. Ah, after a tough day at work, I could use some lomilomi.

lua -- Bathroom, toilet.

luna -- A foreman, boss or supervisor.

mahalo -- Thank you.

makai -- Towards the ocean.

mahimahi -- A dolphinfish.

malihini -- A newcomer or visitor.

mauka -- Towards the mountains.

'ohana -- Family.

'ono -- Delicious, tasty, savory. eg. The laulau was ono!

opae -- Shrimp. eg. They caught some opae to use as bait.

'opakapaka -- Blue snapper.

'opihi -- Limpet. Plucked from shoreline walls and eaten raw. eg. 'Opihi make great pupus (appetizers.)

'opu -- Stomach. eg. Santa got a big 'opu from eating so much laulau, fish and poi.

pau -- Finished. eg. All pau.

pau hana -- Finished with work.

pikake -- A shrub with small, white, very fragrant flowers.

piko -- Umbilical cord, navel.

pipi kaula -- Beef salted and dried in the sun. Broiled before eaten.

pohaku -- Rock, stone.

poi -- A Hawaiian staple made from cooked taro.

poke -- Raw fish chunks mixed with seaweed.

po'okela -- Best, supreme, foremost.

pua'a -- A pig or hog.

tutu -- Grandmother.

'ukulele -- A musical Hawaiian string instrument, introduced by the Portugese.

'ulu maika -- Stone used in playing the maika game (bowling).

umeke -- Bowl, calabash, as of wood or gourd.

wahine -- Woman or women.

weke -- Several species of edible, goatfish that inhabit Hawaiian reefs, characterized by a red color or striped markings.

Index

Meet the Author

Alton Pryor has published fifty-plus books since turning 70 in 1997—many of them about California's past and the colorful characters who rode our trails to fame or infamy.

To date he has sold more than 180,000-plus copies of his first book, "Little Known Tales in California History", and has done respectably well with most of his other titles.

But until fate derailed his 33-year journalism career, he never aspired to write a book, and certainly never anticipated he would come to be regarded as "Mr. Self-Publishing" by his peers in the Sacramento area. "I would have liked living in the Old West," he says. "I wanted, at one time, to be a really good cowboy. I had horses as a young man and even took a raw colt and trained it to work cattle."

But, by the time Pryor was born on March 19, 1927, the era of gunslingers and gold miners was over, and he started life, instead, on his family's farm outside of King City in the Salinas Valley.

He was terminated after writing for 27 years for a magazine. The magazine was sold to a midwest firm. Pryor turned to writing books and says now, "I wish I had been fired 20 years earlier."